The Mad Lender's Guide to Private Lending and Note Investing

Doug Smith

AF850920

First Edition, 2026

Cover art by Addison Smith

Disclaimer

The author of this book is neither an attorney nor a tax professional. The material in these chapters reflects more than thirty-five years of experience in credit lending, note investing, and distressed assets, written from that operating perspective. It is not legal advice. It is not tax advice. It is not investment advice. The discussion of regulatory frameworks, licensing requirements, usury caps, securities considerations, and tax treatments throughout the book is general in nature and is included as operational context. The application of any of these rules to your specific situation depends on facts the author does not have, on the jurisdiction in which you operate, and on developments in the law that may have occurred since this book was written.

Before acting on anything in this book, consult an attorney who practices in your jurisdiction, a CPA who understands your tax situation, and a qualified credit professional who has reviewed your specific deal. The cost of competent advice on a specific question is small compared to the cost of operating on a general principle that does not apply to your case.

The author and publisher make no representation or warranty, express or implied, regarding the suitability or accuracy of the content for any particular purpose. The author and publisher shall not be liable for any losses, damages, or other consequences arising from the reader's application of any information contained in this book.

Preface

This book exists because the private lending market has changed faster than the people in it have. The traditional bank retreat from real estate has pulled capital, borrowers, brokers, and operators into private credit at a scale none of them were trained for. The result is an industry filled with people who know how to find a deal but were never taught how to underwrite one, how to document it so it survives a workout, or how to read a borrower's file the way a credit officer would. This book exists to put that missing training between two covers.

I have spent more than three-and-a-half decades on the credit side of the business, mostly inside community and regional banks, with formal credit training, distressed asset work, and the kind of cycle exposure that teaches you what actually breaks a loan. I now work in private lending and credit advisory, and I see, every week, the same mistakes I watched institutional lenders make across multiple credit cycles. The mistakes are not new. The people making them are.

The book is for two readers. The first is the private lender, whether you are deploying your own capital, running a fund, or operating a lending company that finances real estate investors. The second is the note investor, who is in the same business from a different seat, buying paper that someone else originated and inheriting whatever quality of underwriting was, or was not, applied at the front end. The principles in this book apply equally to both. A private lender lives with the credit decision they made at origination. A note investor lives with someone else's and has to know enough to evaluate it before the wire goes out. Both need the same training.

This book is not a guide to finding deals or to marketing a shop. It is a book about credit. It walks through what underwriting actually is, how to think about character, capacity, and collateral, how to define and price risk, how to document a loan that will function under stress, how to service it, how to manage a non-performing file, and how to build a practice that survives the next cycle. The chapters are written in a sequence, and the early chapters set the framework that the later chapters depend on. The credit chapters reward being read first.

A recurring section called Dougie Downer appears at the end of most chapters. That label is mine, and the voice in those sections is mine. It is the part of the book where I tell you, in plain terms, how the lesson in the chapter looks when it goes wrong in the real world. The reason it is there is simple. The optimist signs the loan. The realist works it out. The realist usually has the harder job, and the realist usually learned that job by living through what the optimist refused to consider. I would rather you learn it here.

Read this book the way you would read a credit policy manual. Read it slowly and deliberately, with an eye toward what applies to your operation. The chapters are short on purpose. The principles are not.

Table of Contents

Part One

The Gap

A gap opened in private lending and note investing when banks stepped back from real estate credit after 2008 and again after 2020. Capital rushed in to fill it. Credit discipline did not. Most of the new entrants to this market are capital holders rather than credit people, and the difference between the two is the subject of this book.

Part One sets the stage. It covers the market conditions that produced the opportunity, the institutional habits that separate a credit operation from a pile of money chasing yield, the mindset a disciplined lender brings to every file, and the thirteen categories of risk that govern every credit decision in this business whether the lender thinks about them explicitly or not. By the end of Part One the reader should understand the environment they are operating in and the mindset they will need before Part Two opens the technical material.

Chapter 1

The Space Most Private Lenders and Note Investors Don't Know They're In

The private lending business in this country did not grow because someone invented a better mousetrap. It grew because banks walked away from large pieces of the lending market, and the capital that used to flow through banks had to find somewhere else to go. After 2008, regulators rewrote the playbook for community and regional institutions. Capital ratios tightened, examination scrutiny intensified, and whole categories of loans that banks had funded for decades became uneconomic to underwrite, document, and service inside a regulated institution. Construction lending pulled back. Investor non-owner-occupied lending pulled back. Loans to small operators with complex tax returns and layered entity structures pulled back. After 2020, the same pattern played out again, accelerated this time by pandemic-era balance sheet pressure and a wave of deposit volatility that left bankers even more conservative about who they would lend to and on what terms.

The capital that used to fund those loans did not disappear. It moved. Some of it found its way into private credit funds, family offices, and direct lending platforms operating outside the bank regulatory perimeter. Some of it flowed into private mortgage funds, hard money shops, and individual investor lenders writing one off loans against real estate. The same forces that grew origination also grew the secondary note market, because every loan originated outside the bank system eventually becomes a piece of paper that might trade. Note investors stepped in to buy performing paper at a discount, non-performing paper at a deeper discount, and re-performing paper somewhere in between. Origination and the secondary market expanded together, and they expanded faster than the population of people who actually knew how to underwrite, document, service, and work out a loan.

That is the space most new private lenders and note investors are sitting in right now, and most of them have not figured out the geometry of it yet. They have capital. They have a deal in front of them. They have a borrower who is in a hurry, and a piece of collateral that looks reasonable on a desktop valuation. What they generally do not have is the training that someone running a credit operation inside a bank would have spent many years acquiring before being allowed to sign off on a loan of any size. There is a difference between holding capital and running a credit operation, and that difference is the entire point of this book.

Holding capital means a person has money to deploy and a willingness to take risk in order to earn a return. That is the easy part. Running a credit operation means having a repeatable process for deciding whether a particular loan is worth making, for structuring it so that it survives the things no one can predict, for documenting it so that the structure actually holds up when it is tested, for monitoring it after closing so that problems surface while they are still solvable, and for working it out cleanly when the borrower stops performing. Most new private lenders are doing the first part well and ignoring the rest. Most new note investors are buying paper as if it were a bond, focused on yield and duration, when the paper is in fact a contract with a human being whose circumstances are going to change in ways no one in the deal foresees.

A credit officer inside a bank is not a salesperson. The salesperson at a bank is the loan officer or the relationship manager, the person whose job is to bring deals in. The credit officer plays the opposite role. The credit officer's job is to test the deal against the bank's policy, against the loan committee's appetite, and against the credit officer's own training. The credit officer evaluates the borrower's character, capacity, and collateral. The credit officer scrutinizes the assumptions in the underwriting. The credit officer asks what happens if the borrower's income drops, if the collateral value drops, if the construction project runs over, if the takeout financing falls through, or if the guarantor's other businesses get into trouble at the same time. The credit officer remembers every loan the bank ever made that went sideways for a reason no one had thought to ask about. In a properly run bank, the credit officer can kill a deal the loan officer wants to do, and that decision stands unless something unusual happens upstairs.

Private lending, outside the bank system, usually does not have that structure. The same person is often the originator, the underwriter, the closer, the servicer, and the workout officer. That person is also, in many cases, the source of the capital. There is no credit officer playing the opposite role because that role does not exist in private lending. The discipline that used to live in a separate function inside a bank now has to live inside one person's head, or it does not live anywhere. When it does not live anywhere, the loan still gets made, the note still gets bought, and the money still goes out. The discipline gap does not show up at closing. It shows up six months later, or eighteen months later, when the loan stops performing and the lender discovers that the documents do not say what the lender thought they said, that the collateral is not where the lender thought it was, or that the borrower is a person the lender never actually understood.

I run into two kinds of new entrants more than any others. The first is the real estate operator who drifted into lending. This person has bought and sold dozens of properties, knows their market cold, understands construction, and recognizes what a good deal looks like from the equity side. When a borrower comes to them needing a loan, they look at the collateral, recognize the property type, do the math on loan to value, and write the check. They are underwriting the property, not the borrower. They are using their own equity playbook to make a credit decision, and the two playbooks are not the same. The equity investor's downside is bounded by what they paid for the property. The lender's downside is bounded by whether the borrower performs, whether the collateral holds its value, whether the documents are enforceable, and whether the lender has the time, money, and stomach to take the property back and resell it when things go wrong. Those are not the same questions, and the equity playbook does not contain the answers.

The second is the yield-oriented investor who treats a loan or a note the way they would treat a bond. This person often comes from a financial planning background, sometimes from a corporate finance background. They evaluate the loan or the note in terms of coupon, duration, and credit spread. They build a spreadsheet. They calculate the yield to maturity. They model the return on equity if they layer in leverage. What they typically do not model, because they have not been trained to model it, is the human being on the other side of the contract. A bond is an obligation of an issuer with audited financials, a credit rating, and a market that prices the paper every day. A private loan is an obligation of a borrower whose financials are whatever the borrower says they are, whose credit rating is a FICO score that may or may not reflect current reality, and whose paper does not trade in any liquid market. The yield-oriented investor often discovers, well after funding, that the coupon they were promised is contingent on a long list of human behaviors, none of which are guaranteed.

I watched a version of this lesson play out early in my commercial banking career, and the seat I had for it was a front row one. Community bank boards, for those who have not sat on one, are not selected for banking expertise. Board members are usually selected because they are connected in the community and because they are expected, formally or informally, to refer business to the bank. That is the unspoken part of community banking. The members who bring in the most deposits and the most loans tend to be the most popular at board meetings, and whether the loans they refer are any good is a separate question.

One of the board members at a bank where I was a commercial lender was a genuinely good man and a productive referral source. He brought a client in to see me about a one million dollar business loan. The borrower was likable, the project sounded reasonable, and the board member clearly expected the loan to get done because he had walked the borrower through the front door himself. When I worked through the file, the loan did not qualify. It did not come close to qualifying. Cash flow was insufficient to service the proposed debt, the projections were optimistic in places that mattered, and the collateral coverage was thin. I declined the loan. The board member was not happy. He went to the bank president and pressed the issue. The president read the file, walked through it with me, and backed my decision. The loan stayed declined.

That should have been the end of the story, and it was not. The board member, angry that the bank would not lend to a borrower he had personally vouched for, reached into his own pocket and made the loan himself with his own funds. He had the capital. He had the conviction. He believed the borrower more than he believed the file. He funded the loan, and he lost the entire thing.

That is the experience I am writing this book against. The board member was not a stupid man. He was a successful businessman with real money to deploy and good instincts in his own line of work. What he did not have was credit training. He was a capital holder, not a credit officer, and the gap between those two roles cost him a million dollars. The bank declined the loan for the same reasons he would have declined it himself if he had been trained to read the file the way the bank read it. The file said what it said. He chose not to read it that way because he had already decided what he wanted the outcome to be.

There is an old line from the poker table. If you have been sitting there for fifteen minutes and you do not know who the patsy is, you are the patsy. That is the line I want every new private lender and every new note investor to keep in mind as they read this book. Lending and note investing look easy from the outside because the mechanics are easy. The lender wires the money, collects the payments, and forecloses if the borrower stops paying. The hard part is the part nobody can see until they have been in the seat long enough to learn what to look for, and the cost of learning it on the job is paid in lost principal.

This book is not going to turn any reader into a credit officer in three hundred pages. Five to ten years of supervised underwriting, loan committee experience, workout exposure, and watching deals go sideways in slow motion is what makes a credit officer, and there is no shortcut. What this book can do is give a serious reader the vocabulary, the questions, the structural habits, and the failure modes that a properly trained credit officer carries into every deal. It can show how a loan is supposed to be underwritten, structured, documented, monitored, and worked out. It can show how a note is supposed to be evaluated before it is purchased and how a portfolio of notes is supposed to be managed after it is purchased. It can show, through real cases and real patterns, what goes wrong, why it goes wrong, and what an experienced lender does about it.

The premise is simple. Most private lenders and note investors are smart, capitalized people who have not been trained as credit officers and do not yet know what they do not know. The market they are operating in rewards capital deployment in good times and punishes it in bad ones, and the difference between the two outcomes is mostly determined by the credit work done before the money goes out. Underwriting is the business. Rate is not the business. Volume is not the business. Marketing is not the business. The discipline of deciding which loans to make and which to pass on is the business, and everything else is downstream of that decision.

Dougie Downer

Every loan looks good the day you fund it. Every note looks good the day you wire for it. The file tells you what is going to happen. The work is in learning how to read it.

Chapter 2

Underwriting IS the Business

The credit decision IS the product. Rate is the way the product gets priced. Every dollar of return a private lender or a note investor believes they earn through pricing can be surrendered many times over by a single poor credit judgment, which means the work that actually drives long-term returns happens before the loan is funded or the note is purchased. That work is underwriting. It is not the most visible part of the business and it is not the part that produces the marketing material, but it is the part that determines whether a portfolio compounds over time or quietly bleeds principal through losses no one modeled in advance.

Underwriting is widely misunderstood as a checklist. New private lenders sometimes ask for a one-page underwriting form, a borrower scorecard, or a list of minimum requirements that, if met, allow the deal to clear. Those tools exist inside banks and they exist inside well-run private lending operations, but the forms themselves are not underwriting. They are but some of the tools of underwriting. Underwriting is a structured judgment process applied consistently to every deal, in which the lender forms a view of the borrower's character, capacity, and collateral, tests that view against the structure of the proposed loan, and decides whether the deal is worth doing on the terms in front of them. The checklist is simply a tool in that process. It is not the process itself. Heck, I don't even use a checklist for underwriting anymore because over three-and-a-half decades that "checklist" has become hard wired into my brain.

The distinction matters because a checklist of some other form can be completed without thinking, and a judgment process cannot. A new lender who works from a checklist will fund every loan that fills in the boxes, including loans that any experienced credit officer would have walked away from out of the gate. The boxes do not capture the essence of a deal. They capture only the elements the form happened to think to ask about, and the elements that decide a loan's outcome are often the ones a form does not capture.

The discipline I am writing about comes from doing the work. It comes from the years I spent inside community and regional banks, where every loan I touched went through a credit officer who was not me, every deal above a threshold went to loan committee, and every loan I made was reviewed annually by people whose only job was to find what I had missed. It comes from the distressed asset work that followed, where the files on my desk were not loans I had originated but loans someone else had, and the job was to figure out why a loan had failed and what the original lender could have done differently before it failed. It comes from the years since, running Castle Rock Capital Funding, where the same discipline that worked inside a bank with second signatures and committee oversight had to be reduced to a process a smaller team could execute without losing focus.

That arc is the reason the book is structured the way it is. The institutional credit discipline described in these chapters is the actual working method of underwriters who learned the business inside regulated institutions, and it is the method that, with some adaptation, transfers to a private lender's desk or a note investor's portfolio. The adaptation is necessary because a private lender does not have a separate credit department, a loan committee that meets weekly, or a regulator coming through twice a year. The lender has to carry that structure inside the operation themselves.

Institutional credit discipline works for four reasons that are worth naming directly. Separation of sales and credit ensures that the person bringing the deal in is not the only person deciding whether the deal gets done. Documented decision-making means that every approval and every decline has a written rationale, which over time creates a record of how the institution has thought about similar deals and forces consistency across the portfolio. Second signatures put another set of eyes on every loan above a meaningful size, which catches the errors or unconscious bias that a single underwriter, working alone and under deadline, will miss. Monitored exposure means that loans are reviewed after closing, on a defined schedule, against the assumptions that supported the original approval, which surfaces problems while they are still solvable. None of these four are about headcount. They are about posture and process.

A private lender or a note investor working alone, or with a small team, can replicate the substance of those four disciplines without rebuilding a bank. Separation of sales and credit becomes a personal habit of separating the role of the person who wants to do the deal from the role of the person who has to defend the deal under stress, and then consciously sitting in the second chair before approving. Documented decision-making becomes a written underwriting memo, even a short one, that explains why the deal was approved or declined and what the lender is relying on to be true. Second signatures become a trusted second reader, a colleague, an advisor, or an outside underwriter, who reviews every loan above a defined size before funds are wired. Monitored exposure becomes a calendared review of every active loan against the assumptions that supported the original decision, at intervals tight enough to catch deterioration while there is still time to act. None of this requires a building or a department. It requires that the lender decide the discipline matters more than the convenience of skipping it.

I learned how easily the discipline gets skipped during the first month of my career, in the most direct way possible. I had taken a job out of college at a consumer finance company in St. Louis, Missouri. I was a baby lender, barely a month into the work, and I had not yet learned what experienced lenders look for in the people who walk through the door. One morning a well-dressed gentleman came in to apply for a loan. He introduced himself as a pastor, and roughly every other phrase out of his mouth was a "God bless you." I grew up in a religious Christian family and remain a man of faith to this day. I am not shy about my faith, and I also do not like seeing it used as a sales tactic or worn for show. In the moment, though, I was new enough to the business that I was taken in by his manner. He was personable and polished, he carried himself as a man of God, and the amount he was applying for was well within the range the company would routinely approve for a borrower of his apparent profile.

Then I pulled the credit report. The gentleman had never paid a bill he had ever taken out in his life. Every account on the report was either in collection or charged off, and the pattern was consistent enough that there was no plausible explanation rooted in temporary hardship. I sat with the report for a long minute, confused, and then I walked it into my manager's office. I told him I did not know what to do because the file was a clear decline but the borrower was a pastor. My manager looked up, looked at the report, looked at me, and said, "what's the problem, just decline the loan." I said, with absolute sincerity, "but he's a pastor."

There was a pause that felt longer than it probably was. Then my manager started laughing. He told me to go decline the loan and come back so he could tell me how the world actually works. I declined the loan, the gentleman's "God bless you's" instantly turned into language I will not reproduce here, and he stormed out of the office. When I came back, my manager explained that the company had run a statistical study some time before on the best and worst paying loan profiles in its portfolio. The best-paying group, statistically, was registered nurses. The worst-paying group, and it was not close, was clergy. The reason, as my manager explained it, was not that men and women of faith are dishonest, because most are not. The reason was that the cloth attracts a small but persistent population of operators who use it as cover, and the people who get hurt by those operators are very often the most trusting people in the operator's circle, which in many cases are little old ladies who had given their savings to someone they trusted because of a title.

I have thought about that morning many times in the years since. The lesson I took from it was not about clergy. The lesson was that a credit decision cannot be made based on a feeling that the borrower is a good person. The file tells the truth about how a borrower has handled credit in the past. The cloth, the suit, the firm handshake, the introduction from a board member, the personal connection, and the warm conversation in the office are all signals, but they are not the real story. An underwriter who funds a loan because the borrower seemed like a good person is not underwriting. The underwriter is hoping, and hope is not a legitimate reason for approving a loan.

That early lesson is what the rest of the book is built around. Every chapter that follows describes some piece of the discipline that replaces hope with solid decisions and turns them into a portfolio that can survive a down-cycle. The pieces are not glamorous. They are documents, internal processes, second sets of eyes, written rationales, and the habit of declining deals that do not work. As you'll hear from me often, "No is an answer." The discipline is unspectacular by design. Returns in private lending and note investing are not made in the funding ceremony itself. They are made in the long run of disciplined decisions that, taken one at a time, do not look like much, and that together produce the kind of portfolio a lender can sleep on.

Dougie Downer

Returns are made by the losses you do not take. The lender or the note buyer who cannot decline a deal is not functioning as a true credit professional.

Chapter 3

What Professional Credit Discipline Adds

The mechanics of a private loan or a note purchase are not hard to learn. The intake form, the term sheet, the title commitment, the closing instructions, the assignment of mortgage, the servicing setup, and the cash flow tracking are all teachable in a weekend if the goal is to recognize what each document does and where it sits in the file. A reader can complete that part of the education on their own with a stack of sample documents and a good outline. The mechanics are not what determines whether a lender or note investor survives a cycle. Professional credit discipline IS what determines that, and this chapter is about what professional credit discipline looks like in practice.

Credit discipline is not the same as transactional knowledge. Transactional knowledge is what a paralegal, a closing agent, or an experienced borrower can possess. Credit discipline is what an underwriter who has worked thousands of files possesses. The difference is the judgment behind the document. The note and the mortgage do not tell a lender whether the borrower will perform. The underwriter or credit officer does by putting their analysis in the credit file. The credit file is not a list of FICO numbers and trade lines. It is a behavioral record of how a specific human being has handled credit obligations across years, what they did when their backs were against the wall, and what patterns we see repeating. Reading that record well is a skill that takes a career to develop, because the patterns only become legible after the reader has seen enough of them, in enough contexts, to know what good and bad behavior actually look like across cycles.

A short list of the skills that take a career to develop will give the reader a sense of what is being claimed. Reading a credit bureau file as a behavioral record rather than as a score. Mapping the borrower's actual sources of repayment, in order, against the actual obligations the loan creates. Analyzing the borrower's liquidity by asking what happens to that liquidity under three or four common stress paths. Recognizing when documentation that looks complete is actually thin in a place that might be important later. Managing a loan that has stopped performing without losing the lender's leverage, the borrower's cooperation, or the collateral's value at the same time. None of these skills are taught in a weekend. None of them are taught well by an instructor who has not had the experience or been through the wringer a time or two. All of them are the difference between a portfolio that compounds and a portfolio that quietly returns capital at a loss, several years later.

There is also a layer behind the skills that is harder to teach and easier to spot in person. It is the difference between understanding that a loan can go wrong and knowing what to do when it does. Most new private lenders and note investors can hold a conversation about the things that might go wrong on a loan. Far fewer can explain, in operational detail, what the lender does on day fifteen of a missed payment, what changes on day thirty, what conversation happens with the borrower's counsel on day sixty, what the foreclosure timeline looks like in the relevant state, what the carry costs are during that period, what the deficiency exposure looks like at the back end, and what the workout options are at each step along the way. Those answers cannot be improvised on the fly. They are the result of having been through the process more than once, which is where this chapter really wants to spend its time.

Later in my banking career, I was hired by a struggling community bank as a commercial lending officer. After a round of layoffs and some restructuring, the role I had agreed to take on grew considerably wider.

I was the commercial loan officer, I handled many of their special assets which is the polite name for the bad loans on the books, I served as market executive for a small area, and because I happened to be the only person in the bank with a Series 7 securities license at the time, I also covered the investments for the brokerage customers. A typical day looked like driving from one location to another with one regulatory auditor on the phone going through a file, while a second auditor at the other end of the same room was buzzing in with a different question on a different loan. It was one of the busiest stretches of my career, and it was also the most concentrated education I have ever had in what poor credit work actually looks like inside a portfolio. The previous team really left a mess and the new team was scrambling to pick up the pieces.

The job I want to spend time on is the special assets work. The bank was struggling because of loans that had gone bad after they were made, and a newer Chief Credit Officer had been brought in to clean up the credit situation that had developed before his watch began. He hired me into that effort. There is a saying in the credit business that every loan is a good loan when you make it. The meaning of the saying is that professionally underwritten loans usually go bad because the borrower's circumstances change or because the market changes, not because the underwriting itself was sloppy. The saying assumes a baseline of competence in the original credit underwriting, and in most well-run institutions the assumption is reasonable. In the situation I walked into, the assumption did not hold. Many loans were not good loans when they were made. The lenders who had made them were gone, and a small group of us were left to work out the consequences.

I spent the better part of that time working files that were essentially indefensible. I would pull a file, read it, and marvel that the loan had ever been approved. The cash flow did not support the debt service. The collateral was overstated or had never been properly inspected. There were environmental issues on a couple of the deals. The borrower's financial statements contained obvious internal inconsistencies that anyone trained to read them would have caught inside fifteen minutes. The guarantor structures were paper only, with no real net worth behind the personal guarantees once you looked through to the actual asset positions. In more files than I can count, there was no underwriting memo of any substance in the file at all. Loans had been made because relationships were strong, because the loan officer wanted the production, and because no one with a credit officer's training had taken the time to write the deal up and defend it before approval. The cleanup was painful. Borrowers who had been told for years that the bank loved them were suddenly hearing from a workout officer who needed answers to questions that had never been asked of them before. Collateral that had been valued generously had to be revalued honestly. Personal guarantees that had been treated as a formality had to be enforced. Some of those workouts settled cleanly. Many did not, and the bank took losses that should never have been on the books in the first place.

That experience is the same one I see playing out, in a smaller frame, with private lenders who do not come from a credit background. They do not know what they do not know. They are not stupid people and they are not careless people. They are operating without the training that would have flagged the deal from the start, and they are funding loans that an experienced credit officer would have walked away from quickly in the underwriting process. The losses do not show up right away. They show up some time later, when the loan stops performing and the lender discovers that the file does not contain what the lender thought it contained, that the collateral is not what the lender thought it was, and that the borrower's other obligations were never mapped because no one knew how to ask. The cleanup looks remarkably similar from the inside, regardless of whether the original lender was a regional bank in the late 2000s or a private lender who wired funds last spring.

The second story I want to tell is about lender education itself, because the cleanest way to avoid making the kind of loans that end up on a workout officer's desk is to learn the discipline from someone who actually has real world experience. A while back, a friend of mine I had not seen in some time came into town to speak at a large hotel ballroom event on the subject of making money in real estate and private lending. He and I had served together on industry conference panels years before and had lost touch. He travels and teaches, but he is the real deal. He worked in the business, he made money in it, he took losses in it, and he learned what he is now teaching by doing it. I respect him.

I wasn't attending the event (I was busy running a company), but we made plans to meet at the hotel bar later in the evening after the day's events were done. While I waited at the hotel bar, I started looking at the rest of the speaker lineup for the event on my phone, and I was stunned. Other than my friend, nearly every speaker on the bill had no background in the subject they were teaching. I do not mean light background. I mean zero. There were no credit careers behind these resumes, no servicing experience, no workout exposure, no time on the lender side of a closing table, and in several cases no documented track record of doing the thing the speaker was about to charge a hotel ballroom full of people to learn. Around me at the bar were attendees who had paid real money to be there, talking to each other about the deals they were going to do and the income they were going to replace. They were ready to go out and make a million dollars. The speakers, with the one exception (my friend), did not have the pedigree to pass on the knowledge they were about to pretend to have. They were cashing checks.

There are good educators in this industry, and there are terrible ones. The difference between the two is not marketing budget, stage presence, or the production value of the website. The difference is whether the educator has actually done the work they are teaching, at scale, across more than one cycle, including the ugly years. Before anyone spends real money on a course, a hotel ballroom event, or a coaching arrangement, the most useful thing they can do is open LinkedIn and look at the resume. How extensive is the background? Where did the experience come from? What institutions or operations did the educator actually work inside, and for how long, and in what role? Have they managed through a downturn? If not, are they bringing in someone who has? There is a saying that those who cannot do, teach. The saying is not always true and there are real exceptions, but it is true often enough that the burden of proof should sit with the educator and not with the student. If a reader is about to spend their hard-earned money on a course and then deploy their savings buying notes, doing private lending, investing in real estate, or for that matter collecting baseball cards, the reader owes it to themselves to know that the person they have chosen as a mentor actually knows what the heck they are doing.

That standard applies to this book as well, and the reader should hold me to it. The relevant question to ask of any author or instructor in this space comes in four parts. The first is the credit decision itself. How many loans has the instructor underwritten, and at what level of scrutiny? The second is the workout. How many failed loans has the instructor personally worked out, and what kinds of outcomes did they reach? The third is the loss. How many real losses has the instructor taken on their own credit decisions, or worked through on someone else's, and what did they learn from those losses that they would not have learned without them? The fourth is the cycle. Have they underwritten and managed loans through an economic downturn like the one that occurred in 2007 and 2008? Many people teaching today have not had to face market adversity. You want to learn from someone that has been through the crucible and come out the other side. An author who cannot answer those four questions specifically should not be charging anyone for guidance in this business, and a reader who does not ask those questions before buying a course or a book is taking on a risk they do not need to take. I make an exception for those educators who have class enough to bring in speakers and educators to fill in those gaps.

Private lending and note investing are not complicated as concepts. They are not. The transaction is straightforward, the documents have been refined over decades, the math is arithmetic, and the basic structures repeat themselves across thousands of deals every year. What is hard about this business is not the concept. What is hard is the discipline of executing the concept the same way, every time, under pressure, with real money on the line, while resisting the temptation to relax the discipline when the deal looks good, the relationship is comfortable, or the pipeline is thin. That discipline is what real credit professionals do. It is the layer that turns a simple concept into a sustainable operation, and it is the layer most new private lenders and note investors do not yet have.

Dougie Downer

The most useful question to ask before paying for any lending education is whether the instructor has personally worked out a bad loan. The answer to that question tells you what kind of book or course you are buying. Do not pay it twice by hiring someone to teach you what they never learned themselves.

Chapter 4

Mr. Spock Would Do Well

My wife will be the first to tell you that I am a geek. I am not just the garden variety geek, mind you, but an absolute, total, card-carrying dork of the highest magnitude. I love science fiction. I quote Yoda when the moment calls for it, and I have always admired the way a Klingon thinks about honor. With all of that said, I am convinced that Mr. Spock from Star Trek would do very well in our business.

The reason is straightforward. Spock made decisions based on logic and evidence. He gathered the facts, weighed them against what he already knew, and reached a conclusion he could defend. He was not swayed by sentiment, friendship, or the pressure of the moment. Those are exactly the qualities that build a clean loan portfolio over time, and they are exactly the qualities that emotional decision making erodes.

One of the most common mistakes I have seen over the years is when a lender sets the underwriting principles aside and decides to go with their gut. Going with the gut is another way of saying that emotion has entered the decision-making process. Sometimes the emotion is sympathy for the borrower. Sometimes it is the pressure to deploy capital that has been sitting too long. Sometimes it is the desire to please a referral source who has steered good business your way and is now asking you to look at one that does not quite fit. Whatever form it takes, when emotion replaces analysis, the portfolio pays for it later.

I learned this early. When I was a young lender, still finding my way in the trade, I went to my manager with a file that did not qualify and made what I now consider the classic rookie argument. "But he is a good guy!" My first manager, who had far more experience than I did, walked me through why character alone does not stand in for capacity and collateral. He was patient about it, and the lesson stuck with me to this day. Good people fail to make payments all the time. Pleasant people often present weak files. The job of the underwriter is to evaluate the loan on its merits, not on the borrower's manners. I remember being a little embarrassed in the moment, and I am grateful for the conversation now, because it framed the way I have approached credit decisions ever since.

The discipline that conversation pointed me toward is not complicated to describe, even if it takes a career to apply consistently. The three C's of credit are character, capacity, and collateral. Character takes the broadest measure of the borrower, including credit history and the pattern of how prior obligations have been handled, neither dismissing what is on the credit report nor overweighting a difficult patch from years ago. Capacity is the borrower's demonstrated ability to service the loan from real sources of repayment. Collateral is the asset that secures the debt, valued honestly and documented in a way that will actually provide us with an exit ramp if the deal goes sideways. The standard does not bend because the deal feels easy, and it does not tighten because the loan feels hard.

At our shop we have a saying that I have repeated more times than anyone there cares to hear. Stick to the model. Our underwriting framework was not built on a cocktail napkin in an afternoon. It was built over years, refined through thousands of files and several cycles, and stress tested against losses, payoffs, and workouts that taught us where the edges actually are. Every time we drifted from sound underwriting principles to accommodate a deal that felt right, we eventually wished we had not. Our underwriting guidelines are not perfect, but they have served a valuable purpose for a very long time. Sound underwriting principles keep us focused on the borrower, help us not to flatter the collateral, and keep us from being impressed by a strong personality on the phone.

A football example may help, and it is one that still stings as a Tampa Bay Buccaneer fan. When the Buccaneers selected Jameis Winston first overall in the 2015 draft, scouts saw a player with enormous talent. He had a remarkable arm, real leadership qualities, and the kind of competitive drive a coach cannot teach. The problem was not the talent. The problem was the decision making in the pocket. He often tried to do too much. He would force a throw into coverage rather than take the checkdown, or he would hold the ball one beat too long because he believed he could still make a play. A commentator put it well at the time. Winston would make twenty great throws, but the one bad throw was what everyone remembered the next morning.

Lenders often make the same mistake, and so do real estate investors who are stepping into a lending role for the first time. A capable underwriter learns to throw the ball away when the read is not there. The right play is to live for the next snap. Passing on a deal does not feel productive in the moment, especially when capital is sitting idle and a referral source is leaning on you for an answer. The discipline to decline the deal anyway is what separates a portfolio that grows steadily from one that blows up on you.

Dougie Downer

The borrower is charming. The referring broker is one of your best. The numbers do not quite work, but you ignore sound underwriting principles and fold to the temptation. The appraisal comes in a little light, and you decide the comps are conservative. The credit report shows a recent late payment and you decide to ignore it. The exit is a refinance into a product the borrower will not realistically qualify for in twelve months. I have seen this movie before in every cycle. The lesson is simple. If you stray from sound underwriting principles, more often than not you get beat. Don't stray.

Channeling your inner Spock does not mean becoming a cold or unfeeling lender. The borrower across the table is a person, and the relationship matters. What it does mean is that the analysis happens before the sympathy, not after. The underwriting principles are the principles for a reason, and they apply equally to the borrower you have known for twenty years and to the one you met last Tuesday. If the file does not support the loan, the kindest thing you can do for everyone involved, including the borrower, is to say so honestly and early. As the old song put it, you have to be cruel to be kind. A quick no is much better than a long maybe. People can handle no as an answer. You cannot drag it out.

I have said for years that it is the deals you pass on, rather than the deals you do, that make you successful. The portfolio you build is the sum of every decision you make and every decision you decline to make. Logic and discipline are not glamorous. They are not the parts of the business that make a good war story at dinner. They are, however, the parts that let you sleep at night and that let you face your investors at the end of a difficult year and report that your underwriting guidelines held firm. Spock would approve. So will your future self.

Chapter 5

Risk Defined

Risk runs through every facet of investing, and it runs particularly deep in private real estate lending and in note investing. Before anyone deploys capital in either side of this market, they should understand the full range of risks that come with real estate and the loans secured by it. Whether a deal is originated or acquired on the secondary market as a performing or non-performing note, the same categories of risk apply, and they apply with the same weight. A manager who has been entrusted with someone else's hard-earned savings cannot carry out that responsibility casually. One of the foremost obligations of a fund manager is to protect the portfolio from downside risk, and that begins long before the first loan is funded or the first note is acquired.

How does a lender or note investor identify and manage risk effectively? Experience sharpens the eye over time. A capable mentor early in a career shortens the learning curve, but mastery of risk management is the tuition of this business. There is no shortcut around it, and the operators who try to find one usually end up paying for it the hard way.

Over the years I have come to think about risk in real estate lending and note investing across thirteen categories. They are not the only risks an operator will encounter, but they cover most of the trouble that finds private lenders and note buyers, and they are the categories I work through when I underwrite a new loan or evaluate a portfolio of notes.

Market Risk

Market Risk is the possibility of a downturn in the overall real estate market. It has happened before, and it will happen again. The full Wachovia and Golden West Financial story is in Chapter 9, where the Pick-a-Pay loan structure was built around the assumption that real estate values would always rise. When that assumption proved wrong, the loans failed, the portfolio failed, and the institution failed with it. That, my friends, is exactly why you don't see Wachovia signs anymore. They ignored Market Risk on a single segment of the market and paid the price in billions of market cap.

Credit Risk

Within lending, the most direct risk is that borrowers in the portfolio will fail to perform on their obligations. This is Credit Risk. In the note space, loans purchased on the secondary market are frequently already in default at the time of acquisition. The reverse scenario also occurs, where a portfolio buys a defaulted loan and finds the borrower attempting to reinstate without a credible plan to sustain the payments going forward. Sound underwriting must contemplate both the default itself and the possibility of the borrower's reappearance, because both situations carry real cost. One warning for note buyers I see is that they will start talking to a delinquent borrower, make payment arrangements, the borrower will make one payment, and then they will default again. Doing so starts the default clock again and it might slow your ability to find a real solution. You have to ask yourself if the borrower is experiencing a temporary problem that can be overcome, or if it is permanent and you are only kicking the can down the road. You have to understand your credit risk on your portfolio and deal with it accordingly.

Interest Rate Risk

Interest Rate Risk has more layers than most lenders appreciate. When an investor borrows capital to fund real estate or loans, the spread between the pool's rate of return and the cost of the borrowed capital is central to the outcome, and the math becomes more complicated when either rate is variable. Market interest rates also drive Price Risk, which is discussed separately below. Holding variable rate loans pushes a portion of the interest rate risk down to the borrower, who may not be able to afford a higher payment once the rate resets. Rate movement affects every portfolio, and deliberate planning is the only defense. I lived through a version of this on the lender side not long ago. In early 2021 we saw the lowest average mortgage interest rates this country had ever seen. Sub-3% rates on a 30-year fixed were not uncommon for ordinary borrowers. One reason inventory stayed thin for several years afterward is that those same borrowers refinanced at the bottom and could no longer justify moving once rates moved back up. The next house came with a payment they were not willing to take on. Now think about it from the lender's perspective. If you locked in those loans at the bottom, you cannot call them back when rates rise. The borrower is not obligated to pay you off. You are collecting lower interest income across the remaining life of those loans whether you like it or not.

Inflation Risk

The cost of everyday items, from a gallon of milk to a tank of gas, tends to rise over time. Some periods see modest inflation, others see sharp spikes, and there have even been periods of outright deflation. Some investors accept lower returns in exchange for what feels like safety, but during periods of high inflation a low nominal return may not even preserve purchasing power. Nominal returns can lie. Real returns do not. A portfolio manager who measures only the nominal number is measuring the wrong thing. Your borrowers can be very sensitive to inflation as well, sometimes more sensitive than the lender is. I have watched several builders purchase land to build on, run into a stretch of runaway inflation, and find that construction input prices had spiked so hard the budget that worked on the day the loan funded no longer worked by the time the trades arrived to do the work. That hits the borrower's capacity to make payments, and in the worst cases it hits their ability to finish the project at all.

Time Value of Money Risk

I have reviewed many real estate and non-performing loan investor models that fail to account for the time required to complete an investment cycle when calculating returns. Fix-and-flip operators are particularly prone to quoting profit on a deal without converting that figure into an annualized yield. Earning a given dollar amount in 2 months is a fundamentally different outcome than earning the same dollar amount over 2 years. Returns must always be measured against the time the capital was actually at work, not against the size of the check at the end. As I write this chapter, one of our best borrowers is in the middle of this exact problem. He built a small set of homes on which a contractor did shoddy work, and the two parted ways before the work was finished. He is now struggling to sell what is on the ground, and the homes sit on the market month after month. He projected the yield on the deal assuming a quick sale. The hold he is now looking at is much longer than he wants to admit, and the yield he priced on the way in dips with every passing month they do not move.

Opportunity Cost

Have you ever ordered the chicken and then watched your friend's steak arrive at the table? That feeling is Opportunity Cost. As cash becomes available, the universe of investment options is rarely as deep as it was the day before. Committing capital to one transaction always carries the risk that a better opportunity surfaces shortly after the loan funds. A disciplined manager weighs the deal in front of them against the deals that might appear next quarter, because cash is only useful when it is deployed in the right place at the right time. Ask an experienced realtor and they will tell you that the first offer is often the best. The grass is often greener on the other side of the fence. Of course, the late, great author Erma Bombeck also pointed out that "The Grass Is Always Greener Over the Septic Tank."

Currency Valuation Risk

For managers who work with international investors, currency valuation can move a portfolio's perceived return as much as the underlying assets do. Movement in the exchange rate between the United States Dollar and a foreign investor's home currency often rivals the performance of the investment itself. A manager who ignores that exposure is leaving an important variable unmanaged, and foreign investors will measure their return in their own currency whether the manager is paying attention or not.

Risk of Replacement

Lenders require hazard insurance, and where applicable flood insurance, on collateral property in order to protect against a catastrophic loss of the asset. What happens when a property is destroyed and the borrower has no incentive to rebuild? Most borrowers in that position do not simply pay off the loan. They walk, and the lender is left with no collateral and no realistic recovery. Some investors choose to self-insure rather than carry coverage, and that is a decision with consequences. Risk of Replacement is the possibility that a property securing a loan will need to be replaced after a catastrophic event, and adequate insurance is the only reliable defense. A responsible portfolio manager requires adequate property insurance with the lender set as "mortgagee" with a proper "mortgagee clause" with the tag "ISAOA", meaning "its successors and/or assigns." This allows the lender to ensure that the borrower cannot grab the insurance proceeds and run. The ISAOA part allows the loan to be sold and assigned to another lender if you choose. A good lender who might buy your assets will, during the due diligence phase, require that proper mortgagee clause on the underlying insurance policies.

Liquidity Risk

Real estate and the loans secured by it can be excellent investments, but they are not particularly liquid. Unlike publicly traded stocks, which can be sold through a broker in a matter of seconds, real estate assets and notes require a willing buyer who is ready to transact on the manager's timetable. Properties can sit on the market longer than projected, and notes can take time to move at a fair price. A disciplined portfolio carries enough liquid reserves to cover operating expenses and the unforeseen issues that always arise, because the moment the manager needs liquidity is rarely the moment it is easy to find. I have been doing this for a very, very long time and even I have gotten caught in the liquidity trap. There are times when deals don't liquidate in a perfect "waterfall" like you expect and you have to call an investor to get an extension or raise capital to cover a scheduled investor liquidation. (Definition: a "waterfall" is the timing in which liquidity events occur in relation to scheduled investor liquidations or reinvestment opportunities...in other words, timing the money coming in vs going out.) Having too much capital, on the other hand, is also an issue as "dead money" is not providing you with a return you need to meet profit or investor expectations. Liquidity Risk is a major concern for any investor or fund manager to navigate.

Geographic Diversity Risk

Assume a portfolio is concentrated in a single small geographic area. Now imagine that area is the Gulf Coast during Hurricane Katrina, or Detroit during the decline of the domestic automobile industry. Concentration looks fine until something local happens, and then it looks like the whole portfolio. As assets grow, geographic diversity becomes a structural defense against regional shocks rather than an optional preference. Spreading risk across markets is not a marketing slogan. It is part of the architecture of a portfolio that can survive a bad year in any one place. Now, this sounds all fine and dandy, but smaller investors and portfolio managers might not be able to hold enough assets in a portfolio to provide meaningful geographic diversity. It's hard to spread your investments out if you only have one asset.

Inheritance Risk

How an asset is held and titled has a meaningful effect on the portfolio when an owner passes away or a partnership dissolves. Without proper planning, the wrong titling can produce probate disputes, partnership fights, and frozen assets that drag on returns for years. Planning for the scenario in which an owner exits or an entity dissolves is not a luxury. It is part of competent portfolio construction, and it is one of the easiest categories of risk to address before the event and one of the hardest to clean up after. I recall a borrower who passed away leaving the property to his adult children. The problem was that the children hated each other. A couple of them refused to be in the same room together. A couple of them wanted to keep the property. One was openly impatient about being paid and wanted the property sold immediately so he could collect his share of the money. The estate sat for a long stretch while the family fought over the asset, and the loan sat right along with it. No amount of underwriting at origination would have caught that, but the right titling and the right operating agreement would have made the resolution far less painful for everyone, including the lender.

Price Risk

Price Risk applies specifically to the holding of real estate backed loans. In an earlier era, lenders held loans through to maturity, which kept Price Risk largely out of the conversation. Once loans trade on the open market, the price of any given note moves with rates, performance, and demand. A manager who acquires or sells notes is exposed to Price Risk whether they choose to be or not, and the manager who never marks a note to a realistic price is keeping the risk hidden, not removing it. I can write an entire book on just this subject. It's hard to do and there's a lot of math involved to truly do it right.

Privacy Risk

Originating or acquiring loans means handling sensitive personal information about borrowers. Protecting that information is both a moral obligation and a legal one. Data breaches can do serious damage to a firm's reputation and balance sheet, and the regulatory environment has only tightened over time. A capable portfolio manager treats client data with the same discipline that is applied to the underwriting itself, because a single breach can undo years of careful work in a matter of days. In this day of AI, this becomes more important than ever. I see a lot of loan officers uploading private customer information into AI engines that expose it to hackers and the public. AI can also open hacker doors to your computer when you might have sensitive customer information. You must be careful with this risk as this is quickly becoming a real risk that many people don't even know they have.

Dougie Downer

A property burns to the ground, and the hazard policy lapsed three months earlier because nobody on the lender's side was tracking it. The borrower has no equity, no incentive, and no intention of rebuilding. The lender then discovers that there is no collateral, no insurance proceeds, and no realistic recovery against the borrower personally. Every one of the thirteen risks above has a version of this story behind it. The lender who treats any one of them as somebody else's problem is the lender who gets the phone call no one wants to take. Risk does not announce itself in advance, and it does not wait for the lender to be ready.

Portfolio management is not easy. It demands diligence, foresight, and a clear head when the market moves against you. The thirteen risks described above account for most of the trouble I have seen across multiple cycles, although additional categories are always possible as products, markets, and regulation evolve. Managing downside risk is not one task among many for a portfolio manager. It is the task. Get that part right, and the returns tend to take care of themselves.

Hope is not a hedge. Discipline is.

Part Two

The Three C's of Credit

Part Two is the technical core of the book. The three chapters that follow walk through the working framework an experienced credit officer applies to every loan they originate or every note they purchase. The framework is The Three C's of Credit: Character, Capacity, and Collateral. Used carefully, the framework produces lending decisions that help lenders survive every market cycle. Used carelessly, it produces files that look good on the day they fund. Those files blow up the portfolio later, because the day the loan funded was the day sound underwriting principles were skipped.

Each chapter in this Part takes one of the three C's and develops it at a level of depth that is rarely available in private lending or note investing education. This is the section a lender or a note investor could hand to anyone they are bringing into their operation and say, this is how we think about credit.

Chapter 6

Character: What the Credit Report Is Actually Telling You

Past behavior is the most reliable predictor of future behavior available to a lender. That is the entire reason underwriting exists. The borrower in front of you today is the same borrower who has been writing the same script for many years before you ever looked at their application. The credit bureau file is the record of that past behavior. It is not a guess about what the borrower might do. It IS the documentation of what they have already done, on multiple obligations, across years and through several economic cycles. Lenders and note investors who confuse the score with the detailed record will be surprised, repeatedly, by borrowers who present beautifully and pay no one.

Before getting into the chapter, a note on something the industry argues about. Some lenders teach five C's of credit, with Credit listed as a category of its own, separate from Character. I do not. Credit history is the longest, most detailed paper trail you will ever assemble on a borrower's character. The way a person treats their obligations is the way you should think about who they are. To separate the two is to act as if a thirty-year record of how a borrower handles money belongs in a different file from how the borrower handles other commitments. It does not. Credit is a part of Character, and that is where this chapter operates. The lenders who break it out are not wrong on the facts. They are simply organizing the same information into one more bucket than I need. I simply have a difference of opinion with those lenders.

Reading the Record

The first thing every new lender should be taught is how to read a credit report. The second thing should be how to lessen their reliance on the score on the top of it. I came up in this business before credit scores were the dominant underwriting tool. We did not have a three-digit number to lean on. We had tradelines, which is the industry term for each individual debt the borrower has ever opened, with the monthly pay history laid out in a grid. Every late payment, every charge-off, every recovery, and every account that ran clean for two decades appeared on that grid. We read it like a historical document. The trend was what we looked at, not the score at the top.

When I started, a bank trained me to work each tradeline by hand. We pulled the bureau report, sat down with it, and went line by line. We were not looking for a score. We were looking for a pattern. A borrower with a single thirty-day late on a department store card from four years ago is a fundamentally different file from a borrower whose pattern shows rolling thirty-day lates on multiple accounts every winter for the last six years. Those two borrowers can carry similar credit scores. They are not similar credit risks. Anyone who underwrites only off the number cannot tell the two of them apart, and that is the most expensive mistake a private lender can make.

The way I describe this problem to new lenders is the dogfighting problem. In the original Top Gun, the instructors explain that the Navy stopped teaching air-to-air combat because the missile was supposed to make dogfighting obsolete. The pilots got too reliant on the missile. Then they got into a real dogfight, and they had no maneuvering skill to fall back on. The credit score is the missile. It works on the easy targets. The moment you hit a complicated file, the score gives you little useful data, and you need the tradeline reading skill that the score was supposed to replace. Most of the industry no longer teaches that skill, which is exactly why most of the industry keeps getting surprised by the same kind of borrower over and over.

What you are looking for on the credit report is the answer to one question. Is this a borrower who has had a problem, or is this a borrower who has a problem. Bad things happen to good people. A child falls off a bicycle and breaks an arm, and the household runs up some medical bills. A business closes and a job disappears. A spouse gets sick and the family burns through six months of reserves before the situation stabilizes. These are temporary events, and on a credit bureau report they appear as a dip with a recovery. The dip is real, and you should never dismiss it, but the recovery is what you underwrite. The borrower took the hit, paid their way through it, and got back to the line they were on before. That is a credit-event borrower. They are usually eligible for credit on appropriate terms.

The recurring-pattern borrower looks different on the credit report. Their lates are not clustered around one event with a clean recovery after. They are spread across years. Accounts close. New accounts open. Balances run up. Collections appear. Charge-offs appear. The cycle resets and starts again. There is no return to a baseline because the borrower never had a baseline. The pattern IS the baseline. That borrower will repeat what their credit report shows you they have already done, because that credit report is a record of who they are when nobody is watching. They are the person who leaves their shopping cart in the next parking space rather than returning it to the appropriate place. The three-digit number on the top of the report does not capture which kind of borrower you are looking at. The tradeline grid typically does if you are willing to read it.

The Nature Question

There is an old story about a scorpion that needed to cross a river. The scorpion asked a frog to carry him across on his back. The frog refused, because the scorpion would sting him and he would die. The scorpion pointed out that if he stung the frog mid-river, the scorpion would drown along with him. The frog accepted the logic and agreed to carry him. Halfway across the river, the scorpion stung the frog. As they were both going under, the frog asked why. The scorpion answered, I could not help it, it is in my nature.

A credit report will answer the nature question for you if you are willing to read it. Some borrowers have a nature that puts them back in trouble. They do not want to be there. They do not plan for it. The pattern in the file is the pattern of a borrower who is going to find the same trouble again, because the underlying behavior has not changed, and the credit report is the proof. Other borrowers had a bad season, made the necessary corrections, and the years that followed look nothing like the years that came before. The credit report distinguishes between the two if you take the time to read it.

This is the part of the job most lenders skip. It is easier to look at the score and approve the loan based on that number. The score does not require you to slow down and think about the human being behind the file. The tradelines do. They demand that you ask what this person was doing five years ago, what changed three years ago, what they did about it, and what the trend has looked like since. That is the underwriting question on Character, and it cannot be answered by a three-digit number.

When the Credit Report Will Not Help You

There are credit reports that do not give you enough to read. A thin file with two tradelines is not a credit history. A borrower who has been outside the consumer credit system for a decade, by choice or by circumstance, will produce a report that tells you almost nothing. New immigrants, borrowers coming out of long-term cash-only living, and people rebuilding after a bankruptcy that has aged off the file can all present with bureau reports that the score model cannot reliably grade. The score will still appear at the top. The number, in this instance, will be unreliable, and you should treat it that way.

When the file is thin or unreliable, you do not pretend the score is the answer. You could build the character picture from other evidence. You could build a credit file from utility payments, rental history, or other people who vouch for the prospective borrower's character. I do not recommend you do this. As I mention in other areas of this book, it's the loans you don't make that make you successful more than the ones you do make. Pass on the loan and live to fight another day. There are many reasons why someone might not have a credit file that matches what you might expect. They might have worked with a credit repair company to have tradelines removed. They might be a fraudulent borrower. You just don't know. Remember, you're risking real capital on this loan. In my view, it is not worth the risk.

Explanation Letters

Every credit officer in this country has read more letters of explanation than they care to count. They come in two varieties. The honest ones tell you what happened. The other kind, which is the more common variety, tell you what the borrower thinks you need to hear in order to fund the loan. Both are useful. They reveal different things, and they should be read differently.

An honest letter is short. It states the event, the date, the cause, the resolution, and what the borrower learned from it. There is no defensiveness. The writer takes ownership of what they could control and explains what was outside their control. You read it once, you understand what happened, and you can decide whether the deal underwrites around the event or it does not.

The other kind of letter is long. It is filled with context the borrower did not need to provide. It assigns blame to other parties. It refers to lawsuits, former partners, former employers, and the medical situation of a relative who was supposed to be helping but was not. It is, in other words, a brief in defense of the borrower's character.

The key to either kind of letter is this: can they produce other documentation that supports the claims in the letter, or is there no proof of what they claim? If you cannot prove it, from an underwriting perspective, it did not happen.

Read these letters the way an experienced credit officer reads them. Not as a story to evaluate on the merits, but as a piece of evidence about the borrower's relationship to their own history. People who have actually owned their past behavior do not need to litigate it. People who have not changed how they think about money write letters that explain why every problem was someone else's fault. Both kinds of borrower can be funded by someone. The question from your perspective is whether they should be funded by you, at the terms you are offering, on the collateral you are taking...and can they prove the story.

The Appearance Problem

This is the part of the chapter most lenders find uncomfortable, because it requires admitting that the borrower sitting across from you is doing something to your judgment that has nothing to do with their bureau file. A borrower with a recognizable last name, a clean suit, and a confident manner is not, on those facts alone, a better credit risk than anyone else. Community standing is not underwriting data. The pew they sit in on Sunday morning is not underwriting data. The fact that they are referred by someone you respect is closer to data, but only in a narrow sense, and only if the person making the referral knows their character in a meaningful way.

I have watched this fail in every direction over the years. A pillar of a community who had borrowed against a building they did not really own. A respected professional who had not paid a credit card balance to zero in fifteen years. A longtime acquaintance of a senior officer at a bank who turned out to be running three failing businesses behind the one the bank thought it was lending against. In every one of those situations, the credit bureau file would have told the story. The appearance kept somebody from reading into their credit history.

The discipline here is to apply the same process to every borrower, regardless of how they present in person. Most failures of character underwriting do not come from missing the data on the credit report. They come from declining to apply the data to someone who looks the part.

The Note Investor's Diligence

For the note investor, the character analysis at acquisition is largely done through the payment history on the note itself. The original lender, if they did the job right, performed the character read at origination by reading the credit bureau file. The buyer of the note is not typically pulling a fresh bureau report on the borrower at acquisition. What the buyer does have is months or years of payment history on this specific obligation that the original underwriting could not have seen. That payment history is the borrower's character expressed through behavior on the note you are about to own.

The same credit-event versus recurring-pattern question applies. A note that paid through a recession, a hurricane, a vacancy cycle, or a personal disruption is telling you something about the borrower's actual character that no bureau file at origination could have predicted. A note that paid for six months, missed three, paid again for four, and missed two is telling you something else. Read the payment history the way you would read a credit bureau report. Not as a row of numbers, but as a behavioral record. Look for the pattern. The pattern is the character read.

The Jelly Bean Test

Risk is part of lending. That is the business. Stupid risk is what gets lenders run out of the business. The job is to take the risks you are paid to take and refuse the risks that pay nothing.

Imagine someone hands you a jar containing ten jelly beans and tells you to take one and eat it. One of the beans is poisoned. You have a ninety-percent chance of being fine and a ten-percent chance of being seriously sick. Would you take a jelly bean. I have asked that question to new lenders for years, and the answer is always the same. No. Nobody takes a jelly bean out of that jar. Then I ask them why they fund files with unresolved red flags on them. The math is the same. The poisoned bean is in there. You do not know which deal it is. You ate it anyway, because the jar in front of you looked like every other jar.

A red flag on a file is the smell of the poisoned bean. You either resolve the flag with documentation that satisfies the question, or you walk away. You do not explain it away because the rest of the file feels comfortable. Lenders who explain red flags away are playing Russian roulette with their own capital, and the cylinder fills back up with every deal they close that way.

Character Reveals Itself in the Difficulty

A close friend of mine invested years ago in a business outside his area of expertise. He put in significant personal capital. He signed a personal guarantee on the operating debt. He trusted a partner who turned out not to be trustworthy. The partner ran the business into the ground and walked, and my friend was left holding losses on the capital he had injected and monthly debt service that was, on its own, larger than his entire day-job paycheck.

Most people in that situation file for bankruptcy. The legal route is right there. The accountant tells you to take it. The lawyer tells you to take it. Walking away is what the system is built to allow. My friend did not walk. His marriage took a beating. His standard of living dropped. He paid every dollar of that debt over a stretch of years I would not wish on anyone. He kept his integrity. He kept his credit. He kept his name.

If I were lending money tomorrow, and my friend walked into the office, I would lend to him on his signature alone. Not because of his score. Because of what his score tells me about who he is when I read the story behind it. The hit, the recovery, the discipline, the years of clean pay history that came after the disaster. Past predicts the future. His past tells me he will pay me whether the deal goes well or whether it goes sideways. That is the entire game.

The borrowers who file for bankruptcy at the first hard month are also telling you who they are. The borrowers who go quiet when payments are missed are telling you who they are. The borrowers who answer the phone, who show up in person, who explain the situation honestly and bring a plan are telling you who they are. Trouble is the reveal. Read the report carefully enough, and you can see who has been in trouble before and what they did about it. That is the single most useful piece of information you will ever get on a borrower, and it is sitting right there in the credit report.

Dougie Downer

A jar of ten jelly beans, with one of them poisoned, is a jar you do not eat from. A file with one unresolved red flag is a file you do not fund. The bean does not become safer because the jar is pretty, and the flag does not become smaller because the borrower is charming. Resolve it or decline. No is an answer.

Character does not change just as a leopard does not change its spots. It does not change at closing. It changes over years of demonstrated behavior, and the credit bureau file is the record of whether that change has actually happened. Read the report. Trust what it tells you. The borrower who is going to pay you is the borrower whose history says they always have.

Chapter 7

Capacity: Ability, Ability, Ability

When I was a new lender, fresh out of college, the regional manager came to town for a meeting with all of the lenders. He was a brilliant, seasoned credit professional, and I sat there soaking up every word he said the way a younger lender does when somebody who has actually been through the cycles is willing to talk. At one point in the meeting he said something that has stuck with me from that day forward. The three most important things in lending, he said, are ability, ability, and ability. Can the borrower pay you back. That is the whole question. Everything else is a way of getting to the answer.

I have repeated those words to every lender I have trained in three-and-a-half decades, and the line is as true today as it was the afternoon he said it. Ability, which is the same thing as the second C, Capacity, is in my opinion the most important of the Three C's. Character tells you whether the borrower wants to pay you. Collateral tells you what you can grab if everything goes wrong. Capacity is the C that provides the customer the means of paying the loan back, month after month, year after year, through whatever life decides to throw at them in between. Capacity IS the primary exit. Everything else is a backup.

This chapter is about how to underwrite that primary exit properly and how to keep yourself from being seduced by surface income that does not recur in real life.

Sources of Repayment

When I sit down with a file, I am trying to identify three sources of repayment in a specific order. Primary, secondary, and tertiary. The primary source is the cash flow that is supposed to service the loan in the ordinary course. For an operating entity, that is income from business operations. For a rental property, it is the rent the property is expected to collect after vacancy and expenses. For an owner-occupant on a residential bridge loan, it might be wages, distributions, or scheduled investment income. Whatever the source, the primary repayment story has to be specific, documented, and durable enough to carry the loan through the term you are writing.

The secondary source is what the borrower can reach for when the primary source hiccups. Other income from the guarantor, financial assets sitting in accounts they can liquidate without destroying the household, a related business that produces real cash flow, a line of credit somewhere else that has not been tapped. Secondary repayment is what keeps a temporary problem from becoming a default.

The tertiary source, and to me always the last resort, is liquidation of the collateral. This is the place a disciplined lender does not want to end up. Foreclosure is expensive, slow, hard on the borrower, and frequently produces a net recovery materially below what the file looked like at funding. When I underwrite a loan I want the collateral to be there, properly documented, and sufficient to cover me in a worst case. I do not want to be relying on it to repay me. If the collateral is the plan, the loan probably should not have been made in the first place.

A Note on Terminology and Ethics

There are operators in this market who will tell you, without embarrassment, that they are in the loan to own business. They are writing loans on the expectation that the borrower will not be able to pay, and they plan to acquire the property through foreclosure at a discount to value. In my humble opinion that is extraordinarily unethical, and it has no place in our industry. The job of a lender is to fund loans that are right for both sides of the table. A loan written to take a property from a borrower the lender knew could not pay is not lending. It is theft from a desperate or unsuspecting borrower, and it should be called by its actual name.

While we are on the subject of names, the terminology in this part of the market is used loosely, and lumping the categories together causes the kind of confusion that wastes everybody's time. Private Money simply means the lender is private rather than institutional. Bridge Lending means the loan is a temporary stop gap to carry the borrower from one event to the next. When an investor buys a run down property and rehabs it with the intent to rent or flip, the bridge loan funds the work until the investor either sells the property or refinances into permanent, long-term financing. Hard Money is something different. Hard Money is a loan written solely on the value of the collateral, with no meaningful regard for Capacity or Character. Collateral is the subject of the next chapter, but I raise the point here because making a loan against one of the Three C's while ignoring the other two is not how a good credit operation runs. The borrower needs a clearly defined exit strategy, and a backup, and then a backup to the backup. Capacity is how that primary exit gets defined before the file ever reaches closing.

Nancy Number One

My first job out of college was as a loan officer and collector for a finance company just outside of St. Louis. That is where I met the first of two Nancys I will mention in this book. Nancy was a veteran lender who had learned the trade from the school of hard knocks, and she was hilarious. She picked on me, and I am going to tell myself she did it out of love. For reasons she never bothered to explain, Nancy decided my name should be Tater-Head, and she refused to call me anything else for as long as we worked together. When I eventually got promoted and transferred to another office, Nancy had a friend bake me, and I will ask forgiveness for the profanity here, a shit cake. That is what she called it. It was three tiers of chocolate cake, each tier smaller than the one below it, finished with chocolate icing piled on in a way that resembled something you would not want to step in walking through a cow pasture. She added candy corn for visual effect, and she stuck plastic flies on top. That, in Nancy's vocabulary, was love.

Underneath the humor she was a sharp lender, and one of the more useful things she taught me had nothing to do with collections and everything to do with capacity. We had a coworker in that office who would talk loud and long about how the company was being too aggressive with its lending, but the minute one of his favorite customers walked through the door, he would write a loan for whatever the customer asked for. Do as I say, not as I do. Nancy would lean over to my desk every time it happened and say, "give it to 'em, give it to 'em, give it to 'em, pop." She was not questioning the character of the borrower. The borrower was honest, employed, and intended to pay. She was questioning whether the lender was stacking so much payment on the borrower's back that, at some point, the straw would break and the whole thing would go pop. She was right.

That is capacity in plain English. Even a good borrower has a breaking point. An underwriter's job is to identify where that breaking point is and to refuse the deal that crosses it. The character read tells you who you are dealing with. The capacity read tells you how much weight that borrower can actually carry.

Stability of Income Versus Amount of Income

A lot of new lenders are dazzled by the size of the borrower's income. Big numbers look comforting on a pay stub or a tax return. They are not, on their own, an answer to the capacity question. The more important question is what the income looks like over time. A borrower making $150,000 a year on a salary that has run uninterrupted for 10 years is, in capacity terms, a stronger file than a borrower whose 3-year average is $200,000 but who had a year at $80,000 and a year at $350,000 in the middle of that average. The first borrower is predictable. The second borrower is a story you have to interpret.

The most durable borrowers I have funded over the years were rarely the highest earners. They were the ones whose earning history was boring. Steady. Replicable. The kind of borrower whose monthly cash flow next year will look very much like their monthly cash flow last year because the source of the income has not changed and is not about to change. That borrower can absorb a vacancy, a rate move, a tenant turning over, or a heating system that fails in February. The high-variance high-earner often cannot absorb any of those things without dipping into reserves they may or may not actually have.

When you are looking at a borrower's income, look at the stability first and the amount second. The number on the page is less important than the slope of the line behind it.

Extraordinary, Contract, and Seasonal Income

Not all income behaves the same way, and a capacity analysis that treats it all the same way will miss. Extraordinary items, by which I mean one-time gains, bonus payments tied to a specific deal, insurance settlements, and similar non-recurring receipts, do not belong in a qualifying income calculation, no matter how cleanly they show up on the tax return. Not too long ago, I made a loan for a professional athlete who received an eight-figure signing bonus. Not too shabby, but the shelf life in his line of work is very, very short. He's only one play away from tearing his ACL and that might be the only big bonus he ever receives. Extraordinary items by definition happen once. They are not the borrower's ongoing capacity to pay.

Contract income is its own category. A borrower with a multi-year contract has a defined runway, but the income stops when the contract ends, and the underwriting needs to address what happens at that point. Is renewal probable? Is there a pipeline of replacement work? Is the borrower's relationship with the counterparty strong enough that you would lend against the contract on a standalone basis? The contract is not free money. It is income with an expiration date, and the date is important.

Seasonal income shows up most often with agricultural operations, tourism-dependent businesses, and certain construction trades. The borrower's 12-month income may be perfectly adequate, but their cash flow within any one year can swing month to month by enough to break the loan if the payment structure does not respect the seasonality. A seasonal borrower needs reserves, an interest reserve, or a payment structure that bends with the income line. A flat monthly payment imposed on a quarterly cash flow without any cushion is a default waiting for the off-season.

When High Income Hides Low Capacity

People who appear to have a great deal of money are not, on that appearance alone, immune to capacity problems. I have learned that lesson in person more times than I would like to admit.

There was a well-known attorney in Tampa, beautiful office, practice that was the envy of his peers, and a taste for nice things. Really nice things. He was one of those borrowers for whom remaining checks in the checkbook meant remaining ability to spend money. I sat through more than one conversation in his office listening to him explain, between calls from his assistant, that he was struggling to make ends meet on income most households in the country would consider massive. His capacity problem was not on the income side. It was on the expense side.

A different file, a different lesson, same principle. I was working on a loan for two physician partners who were building out a new office. The first partner was careful with his money, shrewd in business, and the kind of borrower you would write a loan to without thinking twice. The second partner was a narcissist who liked clubs, liked attention, and liked spending money in places where people would notice. I had the loan structured and approved for the two of them, contingent on the file closing in its current condition. Before the deal got to closing, the second partner went out and leased a $750,000 exotic sports car. That ended the loan, because the loan I had approved was no longer the loan in front of me, and the capacity question was a different question with a worse answer.

The lesson in both stories is the same. High income is not capacity. Capacity is what is left after the borrower has run through their expenses, and some borrowers will spend any number you give them. Part of the story is in the credit bureau file. More of it is in the bank statements. The rest you see in how the borrower lives, because how they live now is how they will live when the income moves downward.

Disposable Income and Reserves

My mom is frugal. So was her mother, and as far back as we know on that side of the family, the same pattern shows up generation after generation. We were raised on a simple rule. If you did not have the money, you did not buy the thing. Only now, in retirement, has my mom agreed to travel a little. That attitude is the reason our family squirreled away a little bit of money over the years. It is not because anyone before me made a tremendous amount of income. It is because the people who came before me controlled the expense side of the equation with the same discipline they applied to everything else in their lives.

Capacity is not only about how much the borrower makes. It is about how much is left over after the borrower pays the bills. Disposable income is the part of capacity most lenders do not look at hard enough. Two borrowers can show the same gross income, the same DTI, the same DSCR on the subject property, and have completely different real capacity, because one of them has a household that runs on 10% of the take-home pay and the other one has a household that runs on 110%. The first borrower has reserves. The first borrower can absorb the surprise that the next 12 months will produce, because the next 12 months always produce a surprise. The second borrower is one bad month from a missed payment, no matter what the loan looks like on the day you fund it.

When you underwrite a loan, you are not just funding the closing day version of the borrower. You are funding 12, 24, 36 months of household behavior that has to keep producing enough disposable income to service the loan you gave them. Look at what the borrower has left over. Look at what they have built up. Look at how they handle a rainy day, because rainy days always seem to come.

DTI and DSCR as Principles, Not Thresholds

The industry treats debt to income and debt service coverage as numbers to clear. Pass the threshold and the file qualifies, fail the threshold and the file declines. That is a useful screening tool. It is not an underwriting answer. DTI and DSCR are principles, not program-specific cutoffs.

The principle behind DTI is that the borrower has to retain enough income after fixed obligations to live, save, and absorb shocks. A 43 percent DTI on a borrower with low fixed expenses and meaningful liquid reserves is a very different file from the same 43 percent DTI on a borrower supporting four car payments and a household running paycheck to paycheck. The number is the same. The capacity behind the number is not.

The principle behind DSCR is that the property has to throw off enough cash, after realistic expenses, to cover the loan with margin. A 1.25 DSCR built on aggressive rents, understated taxes, and a vacancy assumption that pretends turnover does not exist is a thinner file than a 1.15 DSCR built on actual leases, scheduled expense increases already baked in, and a vacancy assumption that respects the local market. That number is not the answer. The assumptions behind the number are the answer.

When you are underwriting capacity, the question to ask is not whether the file hits the threshold. It is whether the income, the expenses, the reserves, and the assumptions behind every ratio on the page would still produce a paying loan if the market gave the borrower a normal amount of trouble. If yes, the file usually works on capacity. If you are leaning on the threshold to compensate for assumptions you do not actually believe, perhaps you shouldn't be making the loan.

Contingent Liabilities

Capacity analysis is incomplete without the contingent obligations the borrower has signed onto outside of the file you are looking at. Personal guarantees on entity debt. Co-signed obligations on a child's auto loan or student loan. Alimony. Child support. Notes the borrower has guaranteed for a business partner, a sibling, or an ex-spouse. Any of these can lurk quietly off the credit report until the day the primary borrower defaults, at which point they become very loud and very expensive to your borrower.

Most of the easy ones will show up on the credit bureau report. The harder ones, which are the entity-level guarantees and the informal family obligations, will only appear if you ask the right questions, read the right schedules on the tax returns, and follow up on every passing reference in the bank statements. A borrower whose personal credit looks pristine but who has guaranteed three operating notes on a related business has a capacity profile materially worse than what shows up on the bureau file alone. The guarantee does not service itself, but the borrower will, the moment the related business hits trouble.

One of the cleanest places to find an undisclosed liability is the interest expense line on the tax return. Personal returns usually don't show it other than on a Schedule C. The business returns, especially on a borrower who runs an operating company, show it in more detail. Compare the interest deduction the borrower is taking to the debts the borrower has actually disclosed on the application and to what shows up on the credit report. If the interest expense the borrower is claiming is higher than the math on the disclosed debts would support, there is usually a liability floating out there that the borrower has not told you about. The math does not lie. The borrower either explains the gap with a document, or the gap goes into the capacity analysis as an estimate, or you decline the file.

Contingent liabilities show up most often in borrowers who own businesses, because business owners sign personal guarantees on operating debt at a rate W-2 borrowers do not. I told the story in Chapter 6 of a close friend of mine who invested in a business outside his area of expertise, signed a personal guarantee on the operating debt, and was left holding losses on the capital he had injected plus monthly debt service larger than his entire day-job paycheck after the partner he had trusted ran the business into the ground and walked away. I told that story in Chapter 6 as a Character story, because of how my friend chose to handle the obligation. It is also a capacity story here. The debt was a contingent liability the day he signed the guarantee. The moment the business stopped paying, the contingent liability became a real one. If you had been underwriting my friend for a new loan during the years he was paying that debt down, you would have needed the obligation on the debt schedule or you would have gotten the cash flow wrong.

Ask. Document. Then add what you find to the capacity picture before you make the decision.

The Note Investor's Capacity Question

Note investors inherit the capacity question with the paper. The original underwriter did the capacity work at origination. By the time the note arrives on your desk, that information is at least months and frequently years old, and the underlying borrower has been living a life through that period. The pay history on the note answers part of the capacity question. A note that has paid through a recession, a hurricane, a vacancy cycle, or a personal disruption is telling you something about the borrower's actual capacity that the original underwriting file would not have predicted.

What the pay history does not tell you is whether the capacity that produced those payments is still there. New obligations show up. Income sources end. Business partners depart. The capacity question transfers with the paper, and the due diligence at acquisition has to refresh the capacity read rather than assume it. A note that has paid for

30 months is a good note. A note that has paid for 30 months on a borrower whose underlying capacity has quietly deteriorated is a problem waiting to surface, and the price you pay should reflect the question, not the answer the pay history seems to give.

Dougie Downer

Capacity is not the pro forma the customer provides. It is what's left over to take care of all of the obligations the customer has or likely will take on. Can they pay the loan back is the most important question an underwriter can ask when making a loan decision. That's capacity.

The regional manager was right. Ability is the question worth asking three times. Repeat after me..."Ability, Ability, and Ability!"

Chapter 8

Collateral: The Most Overused Word in Private Lending

Overreliance on collateral might be one of the biggest signs that a lender lacks experience...and it gets them in trouble. A borrower walks in with a property under contract, the value looks great on paper, and the conversation shifts almost immediately to the loan-to-value ratio as though that one number told us whether the deal was a good one or not. LTV isn't everything. Collateral is the last line of protection, not the first. Value, in the way private lenders and note investors usually view it, is not the same as the price the property would actually fetch if you had to sell it under pressure. Recovering the asset is not free, it is not fast, and it certainly is not easy. A lender or note investor who is depending primarily on collateral to protect their investment has already skipped the analysis that would have answered whether they should be in the loan at all. Collateral is the tertiary form of repayment we covered in the last chapter, not the primary form...or even the secondary.

Before we go any further, I have a disclaimer. There is no way to fully cover collateral in one chapter and probably no way to fully cover it in one book. Every state has its own statutes, its own foreclosure procedure, its own treatment of priority liens, its own quirks on possession, its own environmental rules, and those rules vary widely. A loan that is well-secured in one state is a disaster waiting to happen in another, and the loan documents that work in Texas will not necessarily work in New York or Florida. We will touch on a number of things in this chapter and move on. None of it is exhaustive. The point of the chapter is to give you a hint of the way an experienced credit officer thinks about collateral and the questions you might ask before the file ever reaches closing.

Value Is Not One Number

The first place new lenders get confused is the assumption that a property has a value, singular. It does not. A property has several values at any given moment, and the one that is important depends on what you would actually need to do with the asset.

The retail value is what a willing, prepared buyer would pay for the property in a normal market. That is the number the appraisal usually gives you, and it is the number most lenders think they are protected to. The as-is value is what the property is worth in its current condition, with whatever deferred maintenance, code violations, or unfinished work the property currently has. The as-repaired or after-repair value, often called ARV, is what the property would be worth if the borrower completes the planned work to the planned standard. The as-completed value (ACV) is the equivalent term on a ground-up or larger construction project. The forced-sale value, which is the one that matters most when the loan goes sideways, is what the property would actually bring in a foreclosure auction or a quick disposition/fire sale by a special assets group that needs the loss off the books by quarter end.

These numbers are rarely close to each other. A property with a $1 million ARV might have a $750,000 as-is value and a $550,000 forced-sale value, and the spreads grow wider in a soft market. The lender who funded against the ARV is in a different deal in a workout than the lender who funded against the as-is. The lender who funded against retail and never asked what forced-sale would look like is in the worst position of the three. When you underwrite collateral, it really depends on the situation as to what value you use. In many instances, such as in the instance of funding a flip, you'll likely use two values in the underwrite. Most institutional lenders will lend to the lesser of a certain percentage of ARV and a different percentage of Cost for flips. Conventional Loans will use As-Is Values. It really depends on the situation as to which value you might want to use.

The High-LTV Cycle

Every market cycle I have lived through, and I have lived through several, has produced a wave of high loan-to-value lenders right at the top of the cycle. It is the most predictable failure pattern in this industry, and it happens for the same reason every time. Capital is plentiful. Competition for deals is fierce. Lenders chase yield by stretching the LTV because there is nothing else left to compete on. The borrowers who cannot find money at sixty-five or seventy LTV find it at eighty, then at ninety, then at one hundred and beyond, and the lenders writing those loans tell themselves the value is there to support it.

Do you remember when Jim Palmer, Hall of Fame pitcher, was on every television in the country pitching 125% LTV loans for The Money Store? You can take a guess where The Money Store is today. The pattern was the same then as it is now. It was easy money against inflated value, with no real margin for a market move, and the borrower's only exit when the music stopped was to default...followed by the failure of the lender.

As I write this, there are educators charging real money to teach newer private lenders that they should be funding earnest money deposits, gap funding for down payments, and 100% or higher financing on real estate deals. I will tell you with full conviction, drawn from my experience in every cycle I have personally lived through, that the first lenders to lose money in every downturn are the ones who lent at high LTVs. It happens every single time. There is no version of this movie in which the high-LTV lender survives the cycle in better shape than the disciplined one.

If a current educator is teaching that lending for earnest money deposits, gap funding, or one-hundred-percent-plus loans is a sound practice, the first thing to do is look that person up on LinkedIn and read their background carefully. You will almost always find one of three things. They do not have a formal credit background. They were not in lending before 2008. Or some combination of the two. They have not seen what a real downturn does to a high-LTV book, because they were not in the business when the last one happened. They are leading lambs to slaughter. I want you to survive the carnage. I don't want you to be one of those sheep.

Condition, Location, and Exit Market Depth

Three forces together drive what a piece of collateral will actually do for you in a workout, and they are condition, location, and the depth of the exit market.

Condition is the easy one to discuss and the easy one to misjudge. A property that needs work is not just worth less today. It is worth less in a foreclosure scenario by an amount that is almost always larger than the rehab budget you would have given the borrower to fix it. The buyer pool for a distressed property is smaller, the bids are lower, and the haircut you take to move the asset is real. You have to leave some meat on the bone for a local investor in order to dump it. As a side note, that's how we started rehabbing distressed properties. We were leaving too much meat on the bone for our investors when a deal went South. Instead of fire-selling the property, we sent in our own rehab teams, brought the property up to snuff, and sold it retail.

Location is harder to teach because it changes by submarket and changes over time. The same school district that supported the value at funding may not support the same value when the buyer pool has thinned out in a soft market. A property in a thirty-minute commuter ring around a strong employment center is a fundamentally different file from a property forty-five minutes out, even if the appraisals come in close. A property on one side of the street might be in a different school district than one right across the road. I live in Tampa, Florida. We often see wholesalers trying to justify values for an inland property they are trying to sell by using comparable sales from two streets over. Of course, they fail to mention that the comp they are using backs up to a navigable canal and includes a boat dock...details, details.

The depth of the exit market is the part new lenders almost never ask about, and it is the part that decides how long the property sits when you need to move it. A starter home in a fast-moving submarket sells in days. A specialized property, an unusual floor plan, an oversized lot in a market that does not value land, or a price point at the very top of the local range can all sit for months even in a healthy market. We call such unique properties "White Elephants" and we avoid lending on them. The market for resale on a White Elephant is very limited, and the time value of money lost while the property sits on the market hurts our yield. When the loan defaults, every day on the market is a day of carrying cost, and the carrying cost eats the equity you thought you had.

Lien Theory and Deed Theory States

A loan secured by real property is not the same instrument in every jurisdiction, and the difference is important. Some states are lien theory states. Some are known as deed of trust, deed theory, or title theory states. The legal frameworks treat the lender's security interest differently, and the foreclosure procedures available to the lender are different in each.

In a lien theory state, the borrower holds title to the property and the lender's security is a lien recorded against that title. Foreclosure typically requires a judicial proceeding, with a complaint, service of process, a redemption period, and a court-supervised sale. In a deed of trust state, the borrower conveys title to a trustee who holds it for the benefit of the lender, and the foreclosure procedure can move through a non-judicial process that is typically faster and less expensive.

The practical effect for a private lender is that the same loan, written on the same kind of property, carries materially different risk depending on where the property sits. A nonperforming loan in a state where foreclosure runs 18 months and costs thousands in legal fees is a different exposure than a nonperforming loan in a state where non-judicial foreclosure can complete in 6 months at a fraction of the cost. Note investors run into this every day. When we started buying nonperforming loans in our portfolios, we focused on Deed Theory states like Missouri and North Carolina and we shied away from Lien Theory states like my home state of Florida. The yield that looks attractive on a note in one state may be entirely consumed by the workout cost in another.

When you underwrite a loan or buy a note, know the jurisdiction. Know the foreclosure procedure. Know what the average timeline and cost look like in that state. Build that knowledge into the structure and the price.

Perfected Security Interests

The collateral is only collateral if your security interest in it is perfected. Perfection is the legal term for taking the steps required to make the lender's interest in the property enforceable against third parties and ahead of subsequent claims.

For a real estate loan, perfection means having a properly executed promissory note signed by the borrower, a properly executed mortgage or deed of trust securing that note, and a recording of the mortgage or deed of trust in the official records of the correct county, in the correct sequence relative to any other interests, with the correct legal description of the property. Any one of those pieces missing or misexecuted creates a problem that can range from a small administrative cleanup to a complete loss of priority.

The mistakes I have seen most often over the years are small mistakes with large consequences. A legal description that uses the borrower's mailing address instead of the recorded legal. A mortgage recorded in the wrong county for a property that straddles a county line. A signature missing from one page of a deed of trust that the closing agent never caught. A first mortgage recorded twenty minutes after a competing instrument because the recording desk took the second package first. None of these are dramatic on the day they happen. All of them are catastrophic if the file ever reaches a foreclosure or a title dispute.

Use a competent closing agent. Read what they record. Pull the recorded document after closing and confirm it matches what you expected. The few minutes that step takes are the cheapest insurance you will ever buy on a loan file.

Title Surprises

A clean title commitment is one of the more reassuring documents in a loan file, and it should be. It is also not the whole story. There are categories of claim against a property that either do not appear on a standard title commitment or that appear and get cleared at closing but can resurface later if the work was not done properly. Knowing which surprises wait behind an incomplete or poorly read title search is part of the job.

Junior liens are the easiest case. A second mortgage, a HELOC, a private second held by a relative or a former partner, all of these will typically surface in a standard search. The risk is not in their existence but in how the lender treats them. A first mortgage that is funded without confirming that the existing seconds will be subordinated, paid off, or cleared at closing is a first mortgage that may not actually be in first position.

HOA priority liens are a different and more dangerous problem. In some states, an HOA can hold a super-priority lien for a defined number of months of past due assessments that sits ahead of even a first mortgage. A foreclosure of that super-priority piece can wipe out the first lender's position entirely, and there have been ugly appellate decisions on this in several states over the last decade. If the property is inside an HOA, the underwriting on that HOA's collection practices and any past-due balances must be done.

Tax liens sit ahead of nearly everything in nearly every state. Unpaid property taxes accrue, the taxing authority can sell the lien, and the eventual tax deed wipes out junior interests. A loan against a property with stale taxes is a loan with an unseen senior position you did not underwrite.

Mechanic's liens, sometimes called construction liens, vary widely by state. In some jurisdictions a contractor who provided labor or materials before the loan was recorded can perfect a lien that relates back to the start of the work, ahead of the lender's recorded interest, even though the lien itself was filed after closing. On any loan involving any recent or planned construction, the mechanic's lien risk is one of the questions that needs an answer before funding, not after. In these cases, make sure you have lien releases from the contractors who did work on the property. This is very important to ensure you're in the lien position you expect to be in.

A title search done by an experienced title/closing agent on a property without obvious complications is reliable. A title search done quickly on a property with construction history, HOA exposure, or stale taxes can miss things that show up at the worst possible moment. Read the commitment. Ask about exceptions. Make sure the exceptions you saw at the commitment stage are the exceptions on the final policy...and make sure you actually do get a title insurance policy...not just a title search (also known as an O&E or an Ownership and Encumbrances Report).

Things the Title Search Will Not Tell You

Some of the most expensive surprises in collateral lending do not appear in the title search at all, because they live in regulatory regimes, environmental records, or local political dynamics that sit outside the standard real estate due diligence file. The stories below are ones I have lived through. Each of them taught me, the hard way, something the title search will never tell you.

One of our clients was thrilled. He had picked up a single-story, single-family home in one of the most desirable school districts in the state. He paid cash for the property and came to us for the rehab money. The numbers looked good, the location was good, and on paper everything made sense. There was only one problem, and we caught it during the rehab review. The property sat in a FEMA Special Flood Hazard Area, which meant it fell under the FEMA 50% rule. The borrower could only spend up to 50% of the structure's value on renovations...not the value of the whole property...just the structure value. Anything beyond that and FEMA's regulations required the home to be torn down and rebuilt to current codes. The renovation he had planned was several times that threshold. There are ways to work around pieces of the rule, but his plan was not survivable. He had to strip the project way down and accept a fraction of the upside he had counted on. The borrower did not know about the rule. The realtor did not know. The closing did not catch it. A newer private lender funding that rehab without catching it would have been right behind the borrower in the loss. New lenders coming into this market often do not know what they do not know, and the FEMA 50% rule is one of the more expensive examples.

Take a different file. When I was handling special assets for a community bank, I inherited a loan on a retail center with a gas station as an out parcel. The original underwriting was clean. The property was performing. Some time after the bank made the loan, the underground tanks at the gas station were found to be leaking. The sandy Florida soil acted like a wick and pulled the contamination several hundred yards off the property. The file went from a routine commercial loan to a Superfund matter, with environmental counsel, regulatory agencies, and remediation costs that did not exist when it was originally underwritten. There is a reason careful lenders treat any property with a current or historical environmental use with extra caution. Gas stations, dry cleaners, auto repair shops, light industrial, and agricultural chemical handling all sit in that category. The cleanup cost on a contaminated parcel can exceed the value of the property by a large multiple, and that liability rides with the parcel. In such instances, the borrowers usually walk away leaving the lender holding the bag. That can sink your entire lending practice.

Take a third file, this one a development opportunity. We had identified a beachfront lot on the Atlantic coast in Florida, south of the Kennedy Space Center. About one acre, oceanfront, perfect for three high-end units on the beach. The numbers were strong, and we moved forward. What we did not fully appreciate was that a former county official held a similar undeveloped lot a short distance down the road and was not enthusiastic about the prospect of new competition for the eventual buyer pool. He organized neighbors to oppose the project, the county commission heard our case and ruled in our favor, and we were on our way. Then the private water co-op began having "trouble" providing us a connection (evidently some of the members were part of the original opposition group). The trouble continued long enough that we eventually moved on. In some jurisdictions, even when you are technically in the right, you may not be wanted, and the soft costs of being unwanted are large enough to make the project unworkable. None of that risk is reflected in a title search.

Taking the Property Back

The collateral is only protection to the extent you can convert it back into money. The act of converting it is rarely as fast, as cheap, or as clean as the original underwriting assumed.

Foreclosure timelines vary widely. A non-judicial foreclosure in a deed of trust state may complete in 4 to 6 months. A judicial foreclosure in a slower state can run 12, 18, 24 months or more, especially if the borrower fights the action or files for bankruptcy. During that period, the property is generating no income for the lender, but it is generating expenses every month. Your capital providers expect a return. Taxes still come due. Insurance still has to be carried, often at force-placed rates that are several times the borrower's prior premium. Utilities, if the lender has to keep them on, cost money. The property has to be secured against vandalism. If the lender does not winterize the systems in a cold-weather market, a freeze can do tens of thousands in damage in a single weekend.

Legal costs can be expensive. Servicers and foreclosure attorneys can drag their feet and milk the bill. It happens more than I like to admit and I can't tell you the number of times I've had to call out an attorney or servicer when I caught them padding the bill for a foreclosure action. Add in the cost of REO management once the property is back on the books, the discount required to move it in the local market, the broker's commission, the closing costs on the disposition, and the all-in cost of taking a property back is usually larger than newer lenders expect by a meaningful margin.

Then there are the surprises that wait inside the property when you finally get the keys back. The borrower removed the appliances on the way out. The pipes froze and the kitchen ceiling collapsed. The HVAC system was scrapped for the copper. A relative of the borrower is living in the house, claiming a lease the borrower never disclosed. I've seen people pour concrete down the pipes. I've seen it all. Then, there are some odd things I've seen in foreclosed properties. I remember one where the house was completely empty except for a brand-new, pristine wedding dress hanging in the closet. I guess the wedding never happened. In one home, I found a version of a room you might find in a "50 Shades of Grey" novel. I've seen a lot in my time...and I still am often surprised.

Of all the surprises that come with taking a property back, squatters deserve their own paragraph. They are a real and growing problem in many jurisdictions. The pattern is consistent. The borrower finishes a renovation, lists the vacant property for sale, and a few weeks later a buyer's agent calls and says, I tried to show your listing but someone is living there. The occupants produce a fake lease, claim tenant rights, and refuse to leave. In a number of jurisdictions the police will not intervene, treating the matter as a civil dispute. The legal eviction process that follows can take months. During those months the borrower cannot collect rent, cannot sell the property, and cannot fix the damage the squatters are doing in real time. Eventually the borrower's problem becomes the lender's problem, because the loan is not being serviced and the collateral is being degraded daily. We have seen this pattern repeatedly in recent years. It is part of the carrying cost picture now in a way that it was not a decade ago.

Run the math with realistic timeline and cost assumptions before you fund, not after.

The Note Investor's Collateral Question

Note investors inherit the collateral position the seller had at the moment of the trade, which is not always the position the seller thinks they had and not always the position you will be able to enforce when you need to. The due diligence at acquisition is the moment to verify the collateral, not after you buy it.

The chain of assignments is important. A mortgage or deed of trust travels with the note through every transfer, and each transfer needs to be documented by a properly executed assignment, recorded in the same county as the original instrument. Any break in the chain, an unrecorded interim assignment, an assignment from an entity that had already dissolved, or an allonge that does not match the note it claims to attach to can create a defense in a future foreclosure action that adds time, cost, and uncertainty to the workout. An intact, recorded, in-sequence chain of assignments is what makes the collateral position enforceable. Many lenders never record the assignment, either relying on MERS or allowing the assignments to pile up in the loan file until someone decides to foreclose. Sometimes, it's hard to know who actually owns a loan.

Allonges are the small attachments to a promissory note that extend the endorsement chain when the back of the note runs out of room. They are similar to endorsing a check. Allonges are valid in nearly every jurisdiction when executed and attached correctly. They are invalid in some jurisdictions when they are not physically and permanently attached to the underlying note. A photocopied allonge stapled to a photocopied note by a prior seller does not always perfect what a properly executed allonge would. On the due diligence, look at the actual note, look at the actual allonges, confirm the endorsements run from the original lender forward to the current seller without a gap, and confirm the assignment chain on the mortgage or deed of trust matches the endorsement chain on the note.

One more note about collateral and lien position before we move on to another topic. This time, let's talk about subordinate liens, meaning liens in second, third, or even lower positions. If you are in a subordinate position, you are not just behind the balance of every loan in front of you. You are behind any past due interest, fees, legal costs, etc. if that loan in front of you ever defaults. If you're going to do subordinate lien position lending, like making second mortgages, you really need to know what you're doing. They seem easy, but a novice can quickly lose their shirt if they don't properly understand the ramifications of their lien position.

Dougie Downer

Perfecting your lien position and doing your due diligence before you buy or originate a loan is the difference between you being well-secured and you finding out you have an unsecured loan on your hands. Private lenders often don't know what they don't know...and that gets them into trouble. If you don't know, get professional help, but don't gamble with your collateral.

Underwrite the collateral as the last line of protection. Then build the loan so you almost never have to use it.

Part Three

The Mechanics

Part Three turns from the credit decision to the machinery that holds it together. A credit call that looks right on paper falls apart fast without the loan structure behind it, the documents that will enforce when a borrower stops paying, the closing process that catches problems before the loan funds, the memo that records why the deal was approved, and the servicing function that follows through afterward.

The chapters that follow walk the reader through each of those pieces in the order they show up in real practice. By the end of Part Three the reader should understand the back end of the business that protects every loan the credit officer already said yes to.

Chapter 9

Loan Structure: What Actually Protects You

Sunday evenings were often the time I got a call from my boss saying we needed to have a call on Monday morning at 8am. That meant our bank had just agreed to purchase another bank, and they were telling the officers at the same time they were releasing the news to Wall Street. One Sunday was no exception.

"You need to be on a conference call at 8am tomorrow."

"Who did we buy now?"

"I don't know. Just be on the call."

At the time, Wachovia was riding high. Customer service scores were among the best in the industry. There was talk in the building about Wachovia buying Wells Fargo. That kind of merger would have made us an even bigger player in the banking game. The next morning, I grabbed my coffee, said hello to my assistant and a few of the commercial bankers down the hall, and logged on to the call.

"Great news, we just purchased Golden West Financial."

My jaw dropped.

Golden West Financial was the parent company of World Savings, a huge mortgage lender carrying $122 billion in loans on its book. Most of those loans were the Pick-a-Pay Option ARM product I described back in Chapter 5, the one structured to allow the borrower to pay less than the interest and roll the unpaid portion onto the loan balance. Guess which payment option most borrowers chose.

But do not worry, real estate always goes up. I write that with all of the sarcasm an old credit guy can muster.

While I was still on the call, I logged on and sold the Wachovia stock I held. Then I called my wife and told her we needed to get out now. I have no idea what possessed the people at the top of Wachovia to buy a company carrying that much paper with that kind of structure. Predictably, it sank the bank. Any thoughts about Wachovia buying Wells Fargo disappeared along with the stock price. The market cap collapsed to the point that Wells Fargo was actually able to turn around and buy Wachovia. An ironic twist if there ever was one.

Structuring loans correctly can be the difference between a well-performing portfolio and losing your shirt. In the case of Wachovia and Golden West, structure was not the only thing the institution missed, but it was the thing that was most important. The Option ARM was a product designed around the hope that home prices would continue to rise faster than the negatively amortized balance. That hope was the entire structural assumption. When the assumption failed, the loans failed, the portfolio failed, and the institution failed with it.

That is the lesson I want to start this chapter with. Loan structure is not a foreclosure plan. It is the set of decisions you make at origination that determine whether the loan performs as agreed in the first place, and what remains available to you if it does not. Most loans in this country do perform. That is the truth. Of the loans I have made, bought, and serviced over three and a half decades, the overwhelming majority paid back exactly as agreed, and the borrowers behind them went on to do another deal. Good structure helps that happen. It does not guarantee it, but it stacks the odds in favor of everyone at the table, including the lender, the borrower, and the eventual note investor.

Structure as a Framework, Not a Foreclosure Plan

Loan structure is the framework of terms, conditions, rights, and remedies that govern how a loan is supposed to be paid back and what happens if it does not. The lender writes the loan documents, sets the rate, sets the term, sets the draw schedule, sets the personal guarantee language, and decides where to sit in the lien stack. Every one of those choices does two things at once. It tells the borrower how to succeed at paying you back, and it tells the lender what options remain if the borrower cannot.

Both jobs are important. New lenders, and frankly some experienced ones, sometimes focus only on the second one. They underwrite the loan as if foreclosure were the exit. That mindset has its place in the workout shop, but it is the wrong starting point at origination. The whole reason I do the credit underwriting in the first place is so the borrower can succeed at paying me back. A successful borrower is a happy borrower. A happy borrower borrows again. A happy borrower refers another happy borrower. That is how good lenders build a book.

So when I talk about loan structure in this chapter, I am talking about the framework that lets a good loan stay a good loan. The protections that remain in place if things go sideways are the byproduct of having structured the loan well, not the goal of having structured the loan in the first place.

The Three Sources of Repayment

We covered the three sources of repayment back in Chapter 7. Primary is the borrower's normal cash flow, the source the loan was always intended to be paid from. Secondary is the backup that picks up when the primary hits a bump. Tertiary is the collateral, which we covered in detail in the last chapter and which sits as the last line of protection rather than the first. The reason all three matter here, at the structuring stage, is that the loan structure itself has to fit all three. A structure that fits the primary but ignores the secondary is a structure that will buckle the first time the borrower has a slow quarter. A structure that leans on the tertiary as the working source of repayment is a structure built around foreclosure as the exit, which is the wrong way to build a loan in the first place.

When you sit down to structure a loan, walk yourself through all three. What is the primary, is it documented, and does it actually cover the payment? What is the secondary, does it actually exist, or is it something the borrower is assuring you about? And what is the tertiary, if you ever had to liquidate the collateral, what would the actual recovery look like net of cost and time? A good loan structure takes all three into account. A weak loan structure pretends the primary is the only one that matters, or worse, it bases the loan decision entirely on the collateral.

The Vocabulary an Underwriter

Before we go further, let me put a few of the basic terms on the table. None of this is exotic. It is the everyday vocabulary of any lender who has actually originated loans.

Term and amortization are easy to confuse and worth keeping separate in your head. The term is the contractual length of the loan, measured from the closing date to the maturity date. A loan with a 12-month term matures 12 months after closing. After that date, the loan is due and payable in full unless extended or otherwise modified in writing. Amortization is the gradual paying down of the loan principal through scheduled payments. The word comes from the same Latin root as "mortal," meaning death. To amortize a loan is literally to kill it off. Each payment that includes principal kills off a small piece of the balance until the loan reaches zero. The term and the amortization can match or not. A 30-year fully amortizing loan has its payment calculated so the balance reaches zero exactly at month 360. A 30-year amortization with a 5-year balloon has payments built as if the loan were paying off over 30 years, but the remaining balance is due in full at the end of year 5. Same payment schedule, different end date.

A balloon is the unamortized payoff that comes due at maturity. If the term is shorter than the amortization period, the loan will not be fully paid down when the term ends, and the remaining balance is due at maturity in one lump sum. Old guys like me still sometimes call that lump-sum payoff a bullet, which is industry slang from another era. Bullet and balloon mean the same thing in practice. Either way, the borrower has to come up with the remaining balance at maturity, usually through a sale of the property or a refinance.

A recourse loan is one in which an individual guarantor is personally liable for the debt beyond just the collateral. When the borrower is an entity, the natural person behind it usually signs as the guarantor. If the borrower fails to pay, the guarantor has to. If the collateral does not cover the loan at default, the lender can pursue the guarantor personally for the deficiency. The personal guarantee is the document that creates that liability. Most private lending of any meaningful size includes a personal guarantee, and most private lenders should insist on one. A guarantor who has signed personally has skin in the game beyond the equity in the deal. A note investor inheriting a loan needs to confirm that the guarantee was actually executed and is enforceable in the borrower's state.

Lien position is where your mortgage sits in the order of priority on the collateral. A first mortgage gets paid first out of any sale or foreclosure proceeds. A second mortgage gets paid only after the first is fully paid off. A third sits behind both. Position is everything in a workout. A junior lien on a property with marginal equity is often unsecured in everything but name. Position is usually determined by who recorded first. If a first mortgage refinances and does not pay off the existing junior liens, the new first moves to the back of the line unless the junior lienholders agree to subordinate using a subordination agreement. Note investors should never assume the lien position in the file is the actual recorded position. Confirm it at the county recorder before closing.

Cross-collateralization is the practice of using more than one property to secure a single loan, or using one property to secure multiple loans. A blanket lien is a single mortgage that encumbers multiple properties.

Both are useful tools when the borrower needs more leverage than any one property can support, and both create additional protection for the lender. They also create complexity. A blanket lien complicates partial releases, payoffs, and the borrower's ability to sell individual properties without a workout-style negotiation. Use them carefully, document the release prices, and make sure the borrower understands what they are agreeing to.

A draw schedule is the document that governs how loan proceeds get released over time on a construction or rehab loan. Funds are not released at closing in their entirety. They are held back and released in stages as work is completed and inspected. A well-built draw schedule ties each disbursement to a specific milestone, requires inspection before funding, and keeps the lender ahead of the work. The lender should always be holding more money than the value of the work that remains to be done. That single discipline has saved more loans from going sideways than any other line item in a construction file.

An interest reserve is a portion of the loan proceeds set aside at closing to pay the interest payments on the loan itself during a period when the borrower is not yet generating cash flow. On a ground-up construction deal, there is no income from the property for the first many months, so the interest gets prepaid out of the loan itself. The benefit is that the borrower is not stretching personally to service the loan during construction. The risk is that the interest reserve can become a way of disguising a borrower's actual capacity weakness. If the borrower cannot service the loan once the reserve runs out, the deal needed to be looked at differently from the start.

A holdback is loan proceeds withheld from the closing wire that get released later, typically when a specific contingency is met. A title curative holdback might be released when a particular cloud on title is cleared. A repair holdback might be released when specific work is completed. Holdbacks are useful when a deal can close around a problem that will be fixed shortly, but they require active management.

A holdback that sits on the lender's books with no path to resolution is a problem masquerading as a structure.

That is the working vocabulary for the rest of this chapter.

LTV, LTC, and ARV

Loan-to-value, loan-to-cost, and after-repair-value get talked about almost interchangeably in the private lending world, and that is a problem because they are not the same thing. Each one measures a different number, and each one is useful for a different reason.

Loan-to-value, or LTV, is the loan amount divided by the as-is value of the property today. If the property is worth $300,000 and the loan is $200,000, the LTV is 66.7 percent. LTV tells you how much equity cushion you have against the current value of the asset. It is the most conservative of the three numbers because it measures the loan against the lowest realistic value of the property at the moment of origination.

Loan-to-cost, or LTC, is the loan amount divided by the borrower's total cost in the project. Total cost includes the purchase price plus the rehab budget plus any soft costs. If the borrower is buying at $200,000 and renovating at $50,000, the total cost is $250,000. A loan of $225,000 against that project is a 90 percent LTC. LTC tells you how much of the borrower's own capital is in the deal. The lower the LTC, the more skin the borrower has, and the harder they will work to protect that skin.

After-repair-value (or as-repaired-value), or ARV, is the projected value of the property once the renovation is complete. ARV is an opinion of future value, and any opinion of future value is only as good as the assumptions behind it. A loan of $225,000 against a projected ARV of $350,000 is roughly a 64 percent loan-to-ARV. That number sounds great on the application. It is not actually telling you what the property is worth today. It is telling you what someone thinks the property might be worth several months from now, assuming the renovation goes as planned, assuming the market does not move against the borrower, and assuming the appraiser's comparable sales are still relevant when the project is finished.

All three numbers are important to understand. None of them, taken alone, tells you whether the loan is well-structured. A loan with a low loan-to-ARV but a high loan-to-cost still has a borrower with very little skin in the game, and that borrower may walk if the deal turns sour. A loan with a low LTV against the as-is value gives you collateral cushion today but says nothing about whether the borrower can finish the rehab. The key is in looking at all three together and asking which one to place the most weight on in your underwriting.

A note investor inheriting a construction or rehab loan needs to take the same look. The LTV at the time of acquisition is not the LTV that existed at origination. The property may have appreciated or depreciated. The rehab may be partially complete. The remaining draws may be unfunded. Ask for the most recent property inspection, or better yet, get a new independent one. The partially-completed work might have been shoddy or the property might have been unprotected for some time and it might have deteriorated. Ask for the current ARV opinion. Ask what stage the rehab is actually in. Do not rely on the LTV listed in the original loan documents.

The 100 Percent LTV Problem

Chapter 8 covered the market-cycle reason these loans tend to get written at the wrong moments in a cycle. This section covers what the structure does to the lender once the loan is on the books. There is a corner of the private lending market where loans get written at 100 percent of cost, sometimes 100 percent of cost including rehab, and sometimes even higher when measured against a projected ARV. The sales pitch is that the borrower puts no money into the deal and the lender is fully protected by the projected post-rehab value. That sounds great. The math rarely works out as described.

A loan written at 100 percent of cost means the borrower has no equity in the deal at closing. No equity means no cushion. No cushion means the first thing that goes wrong on the deal, whether it is a cost overrun, a permitting delay, a contractor walking off, or a market shift, becomes the lender's problem directly. The borrower has nothing of their own to lose by walking away. The structure has eliminated the alignment that ordinarily keeps a borrower fighting for their own deal.

The 100 percent LTV problem also reduces what the lender can do in a workout. A loan at 65 percent of value gives the lender room to negotiate. The lender can accept a small principal reduction in exchange for a faster payoff. The lender can grant a brief forbearance and still be well-secured at the end of it. The lender at 100 percent has no room. Every concession comes directly out of recovery.

I am not saying never write a loan at high leverage. There are sophisticated borrowers with strong track records, deep liquidity, and proven ability to absorb cost overruns where higher leverage is appropriate and well-priced. The point is that 100 percent leverage is not a structural feature that protects the lender. It is a structural feature that maximizes the lender's exposure, and it needs to be priced and reserved against accordingly...if the loan is made at all.

Pricing for the Risk That Actually Exists

We lose money on every deal, but we make it up in volume.

I heard a version of that sentence many times in banking, usually said with a tired grin. It is funny because of how often the underlying logic was actually true in practice, even when no one would admit it.

What always baffled me in banking was that some of the middle-level managers in large banks did not know how much the money they were lending out was costing the bank, and yet they had the authority to reduce prices. One of the dumbest sentences you can hear a lender utter is "we will never lose a deal on price." Well, maybe you should. If you do not know your cost of funds and how much it costs you to originate, fund, service, and carry a loan, you cannot price the loan correctly. And if you cannot price the loan correctly, you will quickly find yourself charging less than what the deal is actually costing you to be in.

Cost of funds is what you are paying for the capital you are lending out. For a bank, it is the blended cost of deposits and wholesale funding. For a private lender, it is the preferred return promised to investors in the fund, plus management fees, plus an allocation for the cost of running the operation. Cost to make and carry a loan includes origination cost, processing cost, legal cost, technology cost, the loss reserve you should be building against the portfolio, and the cost of the capital tied up in the deal. Add it all up and you have your true breakeven on the loan. Anything above that is margin. Anything below is a charity contribution.

When the structure of a loan increases the risk, the price has to increase to match. Higher leverage, longer term, ground-up construction, secondary lien position, weaker borrower profile, harder-to-liquidate collateral, longer permitting timeline, all of these increase risk, and the rate needs to reflect a risk premium in the price. Pricing for the risk that actually exists is the right way to underwrite a portfolio. Pricing without accounting for risk leads to a portfolio full of loans that look the same on paper but pay you very differently.

A note investor pays the price they pay at acquisition. The coupon on the note is the coupon on the note, set at origination. The note investor cannot reprice the loan. What the note investor can do is decline to buy a deal where the coupon, with the discount taken into account, does not compensate for the risk being acquired. The price of the trade is the only lever the buyer has. Make sure it is set correctly.

Creative Structure That Serves All Parties

Good structure is not always boilerplate. Sometimes the best loan in the pipeline is the one that required real creative thought to put together.

A historic building sat vacant in the downtown district of a city I worked in years ago. It was a beautiful old building near the courthouse, the kind of property a city's politicians always say they want to see restored, although they often will not compromise on the things that would actually let that restoration happen. A local non-profit stepped in. They wanted to take the building and turn it into a rental office building for law firms, capitalizing on the courthouse location. The problem was that the math did not work. The non-profit did not have the equity to inject into the deal, and a straight rental project didn't cash flow.

So we got creative. The building qualified for two different historic-restoration tax credits. Those credits had market value. We structured the deal to sell the tax credits to investors who could use them, and the proceeds covered the down payment. We also restructured the end use. Instead of leasing the renovated space as a rental building, we set it up as an office condominium so the borrower could sell individual office units to law firms, generating sale proceeds that retired the construction loan. The submission package for that deal was the longest loan write-up I have ever produced in my career. It was bold. It was creative. It was an example of structuring a loan in a way that worked for everyone at the table.

The deal got through credit committee. Then the city politicians changed their minds about what they wanted on that site, and the deal never closed. That happens. The point of the story is not the outcome of one specific transaction. The point is that good structure can be creative, that creative structure can make a deal work for the borrower, the lender, and the community, and that the lender's job is to understand all of the levers available and to use them when the deal warrants it.

Creative structure is not the same as loose structure. Every piece of that historic-building deal was documented, underwritten, and carefully considered. The creativity was in how the pieces fit together, not in how loosely they were assembled. A loose structure that calls itself creative is just a poorly underwritten loan.

Dead Capital and the Waterfall

One of the biggest balancing acts in running a fund is matching the capital in your portfolio to the deals coming in the door. Too much capital sitting in cash means your overall return is dragged down by money earning nothing while you wait for deals worth funding. Too little capital means you cannot fund deals for the good borrowers who want to work with you, and they go find another lender. That borrower may not come back the next time.

I know what some readers are thinking. Use a warehouse line. Yes, warehouse lines exist. Larger operators use them every day. Smaller private lenders, however, often do not have access to warehouse facilities of any meaningful size, and the ones they can get are often more expensive and more restrictive than the simple math of holding deployable cash. So the smaller lender has to manage the waterfall manually.

The waterfall in a fund is the matching of incoming capital, scheduled loan maturities, new originations, investor redemption windows, and operating reserves. Done well, the waterfall keeps capital deployed at a healthy rate without ever leaving the fund unable to honor a redemption or fund a committed deal. Done poorly, the waterfall produces either dead capital or strained capacity, both of which hurt returns.

There are nights even I lose sleep over having too much capital or not enough. It is a real and ongoing problem in this business, and the structure of the individual loans in your portfolio drives a large part of it. Short-term bridge loans recycle capital quickly. Long-term DSCR loans tie capital up for years. Construction loans tie capital up unevenly because the draws come over time and the payoff happens at maturity. A portfolio with the right mix of terms can keep the waterfall flowing. A portfolio with all of the loans concentrated in one duration tends to either flood you with cash or starve you of it at the wrong moments. Construction loans and lines of credit require dead money in reserve that is not paying you interest. That's a major drag on your return. You have to account for that.

For the note investor, the duration question is important in a different way. A note acquired with 8 months to maturity is a different asset than the same note acquired with 36 months to maturity. The yield depends on what you do with the principal when it comes back. Stack the durations across your acquired portfolio the way an originator stacks them in a fund.

Realistic Construction Timelines

Lenders very often set the loan term based on how long the borrower says the project will take or when they want their money back, with no adjustment for the things that actually slow projects down in the real world. Weather delays. Permitting delays. Contractor issues. Material backorders. Inspection bottlenecks. Engineering revisions. None of that gets factored into the term, and then everyone is surprised when the loan goes past maturity.

I think about this the same way I think about Captain Kirk pressing Mr. Scott on damage repairs to the Enterprise. "Three days, sir." "You have three minutes." Scotty always padded his estimate so he could play the hero. Most borrowers in construction lending do the opposite. They squeeze the estimate so they can win the loan, and then they need an extension before the project is half finished. The lender who structures the loan around the borrower's optimistic estimate is asking for an extension request before the project is done.

The trick is to understand the project you are lending on, build the term around what it actually takes to complete the work plus a realistic contingency for delays, and price the term accordingly. If the term you can offer does not match the time the project actually needs, that may be a loan you should not be doing in your particular fund, or it may be a loan that needs a different structure entirely. Pretending a six-month term is enough for a ten-month project does not make the project finish faster. It just guarantees that you will be having extension conversations during the loan.

A few years ago, we purchased a teardown home on a residential island just outside of downtown Tampa. The plan was to build a new construction home that would retail for somewhere around $3 million. The loan structure was set up with a term that, on the surface, looked appropriate for a custom build of that size. What was not factored into the term was the Federal Aviation Administration.

There is a small airport on the island. As it turns out, the FAA requires approval to build any structure of a certain height within a particular distance of that airport, and the home we were building, even though it was only two stories, fell inside that radius. The federal approval process is exactly what you would expect from a federal agency. It is not fast. It pushed the project timeline well beyond the original loan maturity, and we ended up restructuring the loan to align with the actual time the project required.

The lesson is not that the FAA is unreasonable, although on some days you might want to argue that point. The lesson is that lenders very often write loan terms around what they would like the project to take, not what the project will actually take. That project taught me to ask one more question of every construction borrower at intake. What is the single thing about this property, this location, or this jurisdiction that could push your timeline beyond what you are telling me? The answer to that question often changes the structure of the loan before it ever gets to closing.

A note investor inheriting a construction loan with an upcoming maturity needs to ask the same question. What is left to be built. What approvals are still outstanding. What is the realistic time to completion given the work remaining. Do not assume the original term is going to be correct. Build the acquisition around the loan that exists today, not the loan that was originated.

Structure Requires Discipline

The thread running through all of these stories is the same. Loan structure requires the lender's discipline. The credit analysis from Part Two tells you whether the deal is one you want to be in. The structure tells you how to be in it well.

When you sit down to write a term sheet, ask yourself the questions that the rest of this book has been teaching you to ask. Is this a loan the borrower has the actual capacity to pay back? Will it be a struggle for them? Does everything have to go perfectly for this to work, or is there normal-life room in the deal? What is the primary source of repayment, what is the secondary, and what is the tertiary? Does the rate compensate for the risk that actually exists in this deal? Does the term match the time the project actually needs? Does the draw schedule keep me ahead of the work? Is the lien position what I think it is, and is it recorded the way it should be? Does the personal guarantee align the borrower with the loan? Is the LTV measured against a value I would actually accept if I had to sell the property tomorrow?

Walk through every one of those questions on every loan. Sometimes the answers point to a different structure. Sometimes they point to a different price. Sometimes they point to declining the deal. Any of those outcomes is a proper outcome. The bad outcome is the one where you skipped the questions and found out the answers after the loan closed.

Dougie Downer

Structure is not the rope you hold onto when a deal goes bad. Structure is the reason most deals do not go bad in the first place. When the rate, the term, the draw schedule, the collateral position, and the other loan provisions all fit the project and fit the borrower, the loan tends to perform. The borrower wins. You win. Both of you do another deal together. Structure the loan around the loan performing to avoid a default, but also make sure it's structured in a manner that, if it does default, you're protected. Think about two scenarios. What if the loan pays as agreed and what if it doesn't. You have to think about both when structuring a loan.

Chapter 10, Part 1

The Loan File: Core Documents at Origination

Many years ago we agreed to manage a non-performing loan portfolio for a very wealthy investor. He put seven figures into an LLC, and we signed a management agreement under which we would review and place assets into that LLC, manage the portfolio, and deliver him the best risk-adjusted return we could while mitigating the downside to the portfolio. He was excited about a portfolio that had come across his desk that promised, on the surface, real returns. The seller was motivated, the price looked attractive, and the projected yield on paper was within the range he had hired us to deliver. He wanted us to move on it quickly.

We dug into the due diligence. As I worked through the files, I found that the documentation in the portfolio had real holes in it. The problem was not one or two files with a missing item here or there. The problem was a pattern that ran across the entire portfolio. Some files contained mortgages with gaps in the chain of assignment. Other files contained notes with endorsements that did not match the recorded assignments on the corresponding mortgages. Each one of those gaps represented a future workout problem. A number of them were severe enough that we might not have been able to enforce against the collateral at all.

I passed on the portfolio. The client was furious. He wanted me to buy it warts and all. My answer was the same answer I will give in this chapter and the next. The discount is not the issue. The issue is whether you can actually enforce the loan you bought. If you cannot enforce your liens, the discount is irrelevant. He was not happy that I passed, but I saved his bacon by doing so. Whether you are originating private loans or buying a note portfolio, the documentation has to be in order. If it is not in order, walk away and live to fight another day.

The loan file you close on or buy has to be enforceable in front of a judge. The pieces that are missing, signed by the wrong person, recorded incorrectly, or never recorded at all are the pieces your attorney will be asking you about in the first five minutes after default.

That brings me to a piece of advice that I will repeat throughout this chapter. Have your loan documents professionally prepared by a competent attorney who actually practices in the state where the collateral resides. Do not choose an attorney who practices light law. That is a law practice that takes any job just to keep the lights on. That attorney is most certainly not ChatGPT. I am amazed at how many people I run into in this business who tell me they have run their loan documents through an AI tool and consider the work done. AI does not know what it does not know. It will provide you with a document that reads beautifully and is missing the one clause that would have kept the loan enforceable in your jurisdiction. There is an old saying in this business. If you think it is expensive to hire a professional, try hiring an amateur. Hire an attorney who actually knows this type of law and drafts documents regularly. The cost of an attorney to prepare your standard document set correctly is a fraction of what a single unenforceable loan will cost you when you discover the problem in the middle of a workout.

Because this material runs deep, I have split it into two chapters. Part One walks through the documents that get signed and recorded at closing. The note, the security instrument, the personal guarantee, the title policy, and the property insurance. Part Two walks through the documents that govern what happens after closing. The Assignment of Rents and Leases, construction loan documents, insurance monitoring, the assignment chain on the secondary side, collection notes, and the failures that surface most often when something goes wrong. Both parts together describe the file you should be able to hand to your attorney on day one of a workout without flinching.

The Promissory Note

The promissory note is the borrower's promise to repay you. Everything else in the file supports the note. The mortgage secures it. The guaranty backstops it. The assignment of rents and leases reaches the income from the collateral when the deal defaults. The title policy protects your position. The insurance policies protect the asset. The note itself, however, is the debt. It is the borrower's written promise to pay you back, in a stated amount, at a stated rate, on a stated schedule, with stated consequences if they do not.

A correctly drafted note identifies the borrower, the lender, the principal amount, the interest rate, the payment terms, the maturity date, the default provisions, the default rate of interest, the late charge, the prepayment terms if any, the attorneys' fees and costs provision, the choice-of-law and venue clauses, and the signature block reflecting the correct legal name of the borrowing party. If the borrower is an entity, the note is signed by an authorized officer or member of that entity, with the entity name on the signature line and the officer's title beneath the signature. A signature in a personal capacity on an entity loan, or an entity signature on what was supposed to be a personal loan, is the kind of small detail that becomes a very large problem at workout time.

The Mortgage or Deed of Trust

The mortgage, or in deed theory states the deed of trust, is the security instrument. We covered the distinction between lien theory states and deed theory states back in Chapter 8 when we talked about collateral. The document itself is what gives you the right to take the collateral when the borrower stops paying the note. Without the recorded mortgage or deed of trust, you have a borrower who owes you money but no lien against the property you thought was securing the loan. That is an unsecured loan. It is not a real estate loan.

The mortgage identifies the borrower, the lender, the property by legal description (not just the street address), the loan amount, and the terms of the underlying note by reference. It includes the borrower's grant of the security interest, the lender's remedies upon default, the borrower's representations and covenants, the insurance requirements, the tax payment requirements, the use restrictions if any, and the language required by your state to permit the lender to foreclose under the procedure your state allows. Mortgages get recorded with the clerk of the county where the property sits, and deeds of trust are recorded the same way in the deed theory states. Recording is what perfects your lien against third parties and establishes your priority date.

I had a friend who is a divorce attorney call me a few years ago. He had represented the husband in a divorce settlement, and one of the provisions of the settlement was that the ex-wife had to refinance the marital home and take the husband's name off of it. She had done so, but later, my friend got a call from his former client. The husband had received foreclosure paperwork from a large bank on a mortgage against the home that he was unaware of and that he had supposedly signed. When the ex-wife ran short on cash, she went to a bank, applied for a second mortgage, and forged her ex-husband's signature on the documents. The trusting loan officer at that bank let her take the documents home, telling her to have her husband sign them and bring them back. She brought them back signed. The notary at the bank affixed her seal. The bank funded the loan.

When that mortgage went into default and the bank started foreclosure, the husband received the notice and was served. He had no idea any of this had happened. He had not signed the documents, yet his credit was being destroyed. When the bank ran the signatures side by side and looked at the file, the problem was obvious. The signature did not match. The notarization was defective because the notary had not actually witnessed the signing. The bank had been the victim of fraud, and worse, the bank's own procedures had made the fraud possible.

Even after the bank realized what had happened, they tried to keep the husband on the loan. They reported him to the credit bureaus. They damaged his credit. They put him through months of being treated as a deadbeat for a loan he had never signed. He eventually got my friend, the attorney, involved again, and at the end of the day the bank not only had to release him from the loan, they had to pay him a substantial sum for the damage they had caused. The lesson cost the bank a lot of money, and almost all of it was avoidable.

A note investor inheriting a mortgage cannot go back and redo a defective signature or a defective notarization. I call it the sins of the father, meaning the new note holder inherits the bad behavior the previous note holders engaged in. What you can do is look at the file at acquisition, confirm that the executed mortgage was properly notarized, confirm that it was actually recorded, and confirm that the chain of any subsequent assignments was likewise recorded. Many, if not most, files I see have unrecorded assignments. Defects discovered before purchase are problems you can price into your bid or decline outright. Defects discovered after purchase are problems you own.

The Guaranty Document and the Personal Guarantee

The guaranty is the document that puts an individual on the hook for the debt of another party, usually an entity. We covered the conceptual purpose of the personal guarantee in Chapter 9 when we talked about loan structure. Here we are talking about the document itself, what it has to contain, who can sign it, and the practical mechanics that determine whether it is actually worth anything.

A properly drafted guaranty identifies the guarantor by full legal name, identifies the borrower whose debt is being guaranteed, references the underlying note and any related loan documents, states the scope of the guaranty, and sets out the lender's ability to pursue the guarantor directly without first having to exhaust remedies against the borrower or the collateral. That last point is important. Some guaranties read as if the lender has to chase the borrower and the collateral first, and only then can come after the guarantor. That is a much weaker document than a guaranty that allows the lender to go straight to the guarantor at the moment of default. Know what your guaranty says.

On the question of who can validly sign a guaranty, the signer has to have the legal capacity to bind themselves. That sounds obvious. It is not always obvious. A minor does not have the legal capacity to bind themselves to a contract before they reach the age of majority in their state. This is the reason banks will not let a minor open a checking account in their own name without an adult on the account. The minor has a window of time after reaching the age of majority during which they can simply disaffirm the contract and walk away. The infancy doctrine is centuries old in contract law and applies to guaranties as much as to anything else. The same principle applies to people who lack mental capacity at the moment of signing, and in some narrow circumstances to people signing under duress. In any private lending context, the question to ask is whether the person whose signature you are taking has the legal capacity to bind themselves to what they are signing.

This same principle is why a parent who, in common parlance, co-signs for their adult child on a car loan or a credit card is, in legal reality, a co-maker. I cannot tell you how many times we have pulled credit on an applicant and seen a car loan or a student loan showing up that the borrower is not actively paying because, in their telling, I only co-signed it for my kid. The bureau does not care which party considers themselves the primary borrower. Both parties are equally liable. There is no such thing in lending as a co-signer who is not also a co-maker. The same logic applies to a personal guaranty on an entity loan. The guarantor is not a side party. The guarantor is on the hook in the same way the borrower is, just from a different position.

There is also the inverse problem, which is loans to borrowers that cannot have a personal guarantor at all. Private lenders are increasingly asked to lend to self-directed IRAs, either to the IRA itself or to an LLC owned by the IRA. The catch is that the IRS rules on prohibited transactions prevent the IRA owner from personally guaranteeing the debt of the IRA. If the IRA owner guarantees the loan, the IRS treats that as a prohibited transaction, the IRA loses its tax-advantaged status, and the entire account becomes taxable. That is a catastrophic outcome for the borrower and one the borrower may try to blame on the lender after the fact. The same is generally true for non-profit borrowers and for publicly traded company borrowers, where corporate or regulatory restrictions usually prevent insiders from giving personal guaranties on company debt. In every one of these cases, the lender has to underwrite the loan as a non-recourse loan, price it accordingly, and structure the collateral and covenants to compensate for the absence of a personal guarantor. Lending to an IRA or a similar entity at the same rate and structure you would use for a personally guaranteed loan is leaving real risk on the table without being paid for it.

For the note investor, the guaranty is one of the documents most worth confirming at acquisition. Is the original signed guaranty in the file. Was the guarantor properly identified. Has the guarantor moved, died, divorced, or otherwise become harder to find or harder to pursue. Is there a separate guaranty in the file for each guarantor, or is everyone bundled onto one document where a defect in one signature could cloud the enforceability of the rest.

Title Policy

The title policy is insurance issued by a title company against defects in the borrower's ownership and against liens, encumbrances, and claims affecting the property that were not disclosed or excepted in the policy. The lender's title policy protects the lender's mortgage lien up to the loan amount. The owner's title policy, which is a separate policy paid for separately, protects the borrower. As the lender, you should always require a lender's title policy at closing. As a borrower, an owner's policy is usually worth the relatively small additional cost, but that is the borrower's decision.

In Chapter 8 we covered the things a title search does not always catch and the importance of reading the exceptions schedule of the title commitment. The exceptions are the part of the policy where the title company lists what they are not covering. A title policy that excepts the very liens or encumbrances that worry you is a policy that is not actually doing what you need it to do. The exceptions schedule is where the meaningful due diligence happens.

Title insurance is also issued in stages. You will see a title commitment before closing, which is the title company's preliminary statement of what they are willing to insure and on what conditions. The final policy is issued after closing once the conditions in the commitment have been met (typically the recording of your mortgage). Compare the final policy to the commitment when it arrives. Confirm that the conditions you required were actually met. Confirm that the exceptions you negotiated out were actually removed. A surprising number of final policies arrive with exceptions the lender thought had been deleted.

Endorsements to the title policy are a real source of protection or, when missing, a real source of exposure. An ALTA 9 endorsement covers, among other things, certain restrictive covenant violations, encroachments, and mineral rights issues. Other endorsements cover environmental risks, zoning, contiguity for multi-parcel collateral, and a long list of more specialized concerns. The right endorsements for your file depend on the property, the use, and the loan. Talk to your title company. Talk to your attorney. Do not assume the standard policy covers everything.

For the note investor, the title policy is one of the documents that does not automatically follow a loan sale in every jurisdiction. In some states the policy follows by operation of law. In others, an endorsement or an assignment of the policy is required to keep the new lender protected. Confirm the position in your jurisdiction before you close on a note purchase, and require the seller to provide whatever documentation is needed to keep the title insurance in force for your benefit.

Hazard and Flood Insurance

The hazard insurance policy covers damage to the collateral from fire, wind, hail, vandalism, and the standard list of perils. Flood insurance, when required, is a separate policy issued either through the National Flood Insurance Program or through one of the private flood insurance carriers that have entered the market in recent years. Both policies share a structural feature that matters more than most people realize. The lender has to be named on the policy in a specific way, and the language used to name the lender determines whether the policy actually protects you when something goes wrong.

The phrase to learn here is ISAOA, which stands for Its Successors and/or Assigns. The full mortgagee clause on a properly issued lender-payable insurance policy reads something like "ABC Capital Funding, LLC, ISAOA, ATIMA" where ATIMA stands for As Their Interests May Appear. That string of letters is not insurance company jargon for its own sake. Each piece does a specific job.

"ABC Capital Funding, LLC" identifies you as the named mortgagee and loss payee. The insurance company knows to put the lender on the loss payment check in the event of a covered loss to the collateral. "ISAOA" extends that protection to any party that takes assignment of your loan in the future. The minute you sell the note to a secondary buyer, the buyer steps into your shoes for purposes of the insurance policy without the policy having to be re-issued. That said, check with the title insurance company to ensure that the rights are transferable. They usually are. "ATIMA" clarifies that the loss payment is owed to the extent of the loss payee's actual interest in the property at the time of the loss, which is typically the outstanding loan balance.

Why does this matter operationally. Consider a loan you originate with a hazard policy that names you as ABC Capital Funding, LLC, with no ISAOA language. Some time later you sell the note to a secondary buyer. The collateral burns down a week after the sale. The insurance company writes the check to ABC Capital Funding, LLC. You no longer own the loan. You are obligated to remit the funds to the new note holder, but if you are bankrupt, dissolved, or unreachable, the new note holder has no direct claim on the insurance company and is going to be in a fight to recover their loss. The ISAOA language solves this problem by making the new note holder a covered party automatically. It is a few extra letters on a piece of paper, and it is the difference between a covered loss and a recovery battle.

The same logic applies to the flood policy if flood insurance is required for the collateral. The mortgagee clause has to include the ISAOA language. The lender loss payee endorsement has to be in place. The amount of coverage has to be sufficient. As of the date I am writing this, flood coverage through the NFIP is capped at $250,000. On most income-producing properties the lender will require coverage equal to the lesser of the loan balance or the replacement cost of the improvements. On primary residence collateral, the rules differ. Know what your state and your loan program require.

At closing, get a paid receipt or a binder confirming coverage is in force. Get the actual declarations page within the timeline your loan documents require, typically thirty days. Confirm the named insured, the mortgagee clause, the coverage amount, the deductible, and the policy period. File the declarations page in the loan file and tag the renewal date for monitoring. We will pick up the monitoring side of insurance in Part Two.

For the note investor, insurance is one of the easiest places to surface a hidden problem at acquisition. Ask for the current declarations pages for hazard and, if applicable, flood. Confirm the ISAOA language is in place. If the mortgagee clause names only the originator, you have a problem to address before or at closing. Confirm the policies are paid current and confirm the renewal dates. An inherited loan with a lapsed insurance policy is a loan with an unprotected collateral position, which is a different loan than the one you thought you were buying.

Looking Ahead to Part Two

What we have covered to this point are the documents that establish the lender's position at the moment of closing. The note creates the debt. The mortgage or deed of trust secures it. The guaranty backstops it. The title policy protects the recorded position. The insurance protects the asset. If you have those five document categories handled correctly, the day-one position of your loan is in good shape. Part Two of this chapter covers what happens after that. The Assignment of Rents and Leases that you executed at closing but that lies dormant until default. The construction loan documents that govern draws on a build. The insurance monitoring that keeps your collateral protected through the life of the loan. The assignment chain on the secondary side that determines whether your enforcement rights actually travel with the paper. The collection notes that capture what the borrower has said to your servicer. And the documentation failures that surface most often when something has already gone wrong. Part Two is the work the day-one file makes possible.

Dougie Downer

The day the loan closes is the only day the documents are easy to fix. After that, every error becomes a problem and every problem becomes expensive. Get the note right. Get the mortgage recorded right. Get the guaranty signed by the right person. Get the title policy issued the way you negotiated it. Get the insurance set up with the ISAOA language in place. Do those five things correctly and you have built a file that will hold up. Skip any one of them and you will be calling your attorney from a position you will not enjoy being in.

Chapter 10, Part 2

The Loan File: Documents That Govern the Life of the Loan

Part One of this chapter covered the documents that establish the lender's position at closing. The promissory note, the mortgage or deed of trust, the personal guaranty, the title policy, and the hazard and flood insurance. If all five are handled correctly, the day-one position of your loan is in good shape. Your job does not end there. The documents in Part Two govern what happens after closing. Some of them, like the Assignment of Rents and Leases, were executed at closing but stay dormant until the loan goes into default. Others, like the construction loan agreement and the insurance monitoring routine, drive operational decisions across the life of the loan. Still others, like the assignment of mortgage and the allonge, govern whether your enforcement rights travel with the paper when the note changes hands. And the collection notes and the servicer's file are where the real-time story of the loan gets written down. Get Part Two right and the file you built in Part One actually does what you wanted it to do.

Assignment of Rents and Leases

The Assignment of Rents and Leases (let us call it ARL so we do not have to keep typing the long version) is the document that transfers to the lender, conditionally upon default, the borrower's right to collect rent and enforce leases on the collateral property. On a performing loan, the borrower continues to collect rents and operate the property as the landlord. The lender's rights under the ARL are dormant. When the loan goes into default, the lender can invoke the assignment, step into the landlord's shoes, and start collecting rent directly from the tenants to be applied to the loan while the workout or foreclosure proceeds.

The ARL is most often associated with commercial loans, but it belongs in the file on any income-producing residential collateral as well. That includes single-family rentals, duplexes, quads, and small multifamily, or really any property where the borrower is collecting rent from a tenant. Without the ARL in the file, the borrower can continue to collect rent on a property they are about to lose to foreclosure, pocket the cash, and leave you to discover later that the tenants paid the borrower instead of paying you.

We had a foreclosure on a residential duplex in Maryland a few years back. We took the property back through foreclosure, and the very next month the old owner showed up to collect the rent from the tenants. He had not told the tenants anything had changed. He was just showing up the way he always had. The tenants were paying him without realizing they were paying the wrong party. We stepped in and informed the tenants of the ARL and that they needed to be paying us as the new owner of the loan while the foreclosure action moved through the process. That outcome only worked because the ARL was in the file. If we had not had it, the old owner would have continued collecting cash from tenants who had no reason to question him, and we would have spent months unwinding what should have been a clean transition.

A note investor inheriting a loan with rental collateral should confirm that the ARL is in the file, that it was recorded if recording is required in that jurisdiction, and that any tenant estoppels reflect the lease terms as they actually exist.

Construction Loan Documents

A construction loan or a substantial rehab loan brings an entire additional set of documents into the file. The construction loan agreement, sometimes called the disbursement agreement, is the master document. It sets out the borrower's representations about the project, the budget, the schedule, the milestones, the conditions to each draw, the lender's inspection rights, the lender's rights upon default in the construction itself, and the consequences if the budget is exceeded or the schedule slips. This document is materially longer and more detailed than the documentation on a standard purchase loan, and for good reason. There is a lot more that can go wrong on a construction loan, and the file has to address those things.

The draw request procedure is documented either inside the construction loan agreement or in a separate procedures schedule. It defines what the borrower has to submit to request a draw, who has to approve the request, what inspection is required, what lien waivers have to accompany each draw, and how long the lender has to fund. Lien waivers in particular are critical. A lien waiver is a signed acknowledgment from a contractor or subcontractor that they have been paid for work performed through a particular date and will not file a mechanic's lien against the property for that work. Without lien waivers in the file, the lender is funding draws without any direct confirmation that the people doing the work are actually being paid by the borrower. That is how mechanic's liens end up filed against your collateral after the project is finished, even though you funded what the borrower told you was a draw to pay those very subcontractors.

Third-party inspection records belong in the file for every funded draw. The inspector confirms that the work being paid for has actually been completed, that the materials are on site or installed correctly, and that the project is progressing in line with the budget and schedule. The inspector's report is the lender's eyes on the project. Without it, the lender is funding based on the borrower's say-so. We covered the draw schedule discipline in Chapter 9 (the lender should always be holding more money than the work that remains to be done is worth). The draw request and inspection documentation is how that discipline gets enforced loan by loan.

Contractor agreements, while they are between the borrower and the contractor rather than between the borrower and you, should be in the file. A copy of the executed general contractor agreement, the schedule of values, the scope of work, the subcontractor list with contact information, and the certificates of insurance for the general and the subs all belong in the construction file. If a contractor walks off the project or files a lien, you want to know who they were, what they were owed, and what they had been paid. That information is much easier to gather while the project is moving than it is in the middle of a workout.

Builder's risk insurance is a construction-specific insurance policy that covers the structure during the construction period, before the standard hazard policy is appropriate. The lender has to be named on the builder's risk policy in the same ISAOA-style way as on the standard hazard policy. The policy has to be in force from the start of construction. It has to convert to or be replaced by the standard hazard policy at the appropriate time. Builder's risk that lapses mid-construction is a project sitting uninsured against fire, wind, vandalism, theft of materials, and a long list of other risks that all occur with disturbing frequency on construction sites.

General liability coverage on the contractor is another file item that quietly becomes important when something goes wrong. A worker injured on the site, a passerby injured by a falling object, property damage to a neighboring parcel, all of these become the lender's problem indirectly if the contractor cannot or will not respond. Confirm the contractor's general liability coverage at the start of the project and confirm that the borrower has appropriate liability coverage on the property during construction as well.

For the note investor purchasing a partially funded construction loan, the construction file is one of the most due-diligence-intensive acquisitions in private credit. The remaining draws are unfunded obligations you are about to take on. The work completed to date may or may not match what was paid for. The lien waivers may or may not cover the full amount paid. Get an independent inspector on the property before closing. Confirm the remaining budget. Confirm there are no recorded mechanic's liens. Confirm the insurance is still in force, including the builder's risk. The price of the trade should reflect what you are actually inheriting, not what the original loan was supposed to be when it was originated. If I may add my personal opinion, do not lend on partially completed projects. You are taking over someone else's work and all the warts that come with it. You have no idea of the quality of the work. I, personally, would avoid this type of lending.

Insurance Monitoring and Servicing Protocols

The insurance policies in your loan file have to remain in force for the life of the loan. Borrowers do not always pay their premiums on time. Policies cancel. New policies get issued with different mortgagee clauses or with reduced coverage. Without a monitoring system, the first time you learn that your collateral is uninsured is when something happens to it.

A working insurance monitoring protocol does a few things. It tracks every active policy by loan number, with the carrier, the policy number, the named insured, the mortgagee clause, the coverage amount, the deductible, the premium due dates, and the renewal date. It receives renewal certificates from the carrier and confirms continued coverage at each renewal. It flags any policy that does not renew, that renews with reduced coverage, that loses the ISAOA mortgagee language, or that gets cancelled mid-term for non-payment. It also triggers force-placed coverage when the borrower's policy lapses and the borrower does not promptly replace it.

Force-placed insurance is a policy the lender purchases on the borrower's behalf to cover the collateral when the borrower's policy has lapsed. It is much more expensive than the policy the borrower could obtain on their own, and it only covers the lender's interest, not the borrower's personal property or liability. Borrowers do not like force-placed insurance, which is actually the point. The cost of the force-placed policy gets added to the borrower's loan balance, the borrower notices the increase, and that notification typically prompts the borrower to obtain their own policy and present proof of coverage so the force-placed policy can be cancelled.

Many private lenders outsource servicing to a licensed servicer, and the servicer handles the insurance monitoring as part of the contract. Many smaller private lenders try to handle servicing in-house and discover, the first time a policy lapses on a critical file, that insurance monitoring is more work than they were prepared for. There is no shame in handing this work to a professional servicer. It is often legally required. There is real risk in pretending you can keep up with it on a growing portfolio and then discovering you have not.

For the note investor, the question at acquisition is the same one we just discussed for the originator. Are the policies in force. Are the mortgagee clauses correct. When are the renewals due. Who is going to monitor going forward. If the seller has been servicing in-house and you are bringing in a servicer, the transition has to include a clean handoff of the insurance file. Lapses during handoff are common and avoidable.

The Assignment of Mortgage and the Allonge

Let's say the loans get sold and the notes change hands. Whole pools can move between lenders. Every time a loan moves, two documents have to move with it. The mortgage (or deed of trust) gets transferred by an assignment of mortgage. The note gets transferred by endorsement, and when the note runs out of room for additional endorsements, the endorsement gets placed on an allonge attached to the original note. Both documents are essential to keeping the chain of ownership clean.

An assignment of mortgage is the legal document by which the current holder of the mortgage transfers it to a new holder. The assignment identifies the assignor (the seller), the assignee (the buyer), the original mortgage by recording reference, the property, the borrower, the original loan amount, and the date of the assignment. It is signed by the assignor and notarized. Critically, it is also recorded in the same county records where the original mortgage was recorded. Recording is what gives the assignment its effect against third parties, including subsequent buyers, junior lienholders, and a court considering a future foreclosure.

Assignment failures are one of the most common due diligence problems on note portfolios. The original mortgage was recorded. The loan was sold. The assignment was prepared. The assignment never got recorded. The loan was sold again. The second assignment was prepared. It also never got recorded. The result is a public record that shows the original lender still owns the mortgage, while the private files show two intervening assignments to parties that no longer exist or are no longer in business. Fixing that chain in the middle of a foreclosure is expensive, time-consuming, and sometimes impossible. Due diligence at acquisition must show that every assignment in the chain has been recorded and whether the parties who executed each assignment had the authority to do so at the time.

The allonge is a separate sheet of paper that gets physically attached to the original promissory note and carries an additional endorsement transferring the note from one party to another. The original note has a signature block and, usually, space for one or two endorsements on the back. Once that space is exhausted, additional endorsements have to be placed on an allonge to preserve the chain. The allonge has to be physically attached to the note (some courts have been very strict about this requirement), and the endorsement on the allonge has to identify the parties and be signed by the endorser.

The legal distinction between the two documents is important because they are doing different things. The assignment transfers the security instrument. The allonge moves the debt instrument. A buyer of a note who receives a recorded assignment of mortgage but does not receive the original note with the proper endorsement chain (including any allonges) has bought half of what they thought they were buying. The other half is sitting somewhere with someone who can possibly claim ownership of the debt itself. That is not a position you want to be in when the loan goes into default and you need to enforce your rights.

For the note investor, the assignment and allonge due diligence is non-negotiable. Before closing, demand the complete chain of assignments from the original lender to the current seller, with recording information on each. Demand the original note with all endorsements legible and intact, including any allonges, properly attached and signed. Confirm that the seller has the right to convey to you by reviewing their own acquisition documents and their own authority. The cleaner the chain, the cleaner the loan. The messier the chain, the more you should be discounting the bid and the more you should be considering whether to walk away entirely.

Collection Notes and the Servicer's File

The collection notes are not loan documents in the technical sense. They are not signed at closing, they are not recorded, and they do not create or transfer rights. For a note investor, however, the collection notes are one of the most useful pieces of information in the entire file. They tell you what the borrower has actually said about the loan, the property, and their situation. They tell you what the prior servicer has tried, what the borrower has agreed to, what the borrower has refused, and what conversations remain open. They tell you a great deal about borrower intention.

We were doing due diligence on a single-asset note a few years back. The collateral was a single-family residential property that had been a rental at origination. The borrowers, a husband and wife, had purchased it as an investment property and put a tenant in. The note was severely delinquent. The previous lender had refused to negotiate. They were asking for the full unpaid balance plus the deficiency, and they would not entertain any short sale or other resolution short of foreclosure. They had ultimately gotten tired of carrying the loan and offered the note to us at a meaningful discount to the unpaid principal balance, with the collateral itself worth less than the loan.

What turned the deal for us was reading the collection notes. The notes showed that, in the months leading up to our review, the borrowers had gone through a divorce. The wife had moved into the rental property. She had told the prior lender, in plain language documented in the notes, that she was willing to sign a deed in lieu of foreclosure, leave the property in good condition, and walk away if the lender would waive the deficiency balance. The prior lender had refused. The notes did not say why, just that the request was refused and that the file was being prepared for foreclosure.

We bought the note. The first call I made after closing was to the borrower. I introduced myself, told her we had acquired the loan, and told her I had read the file including the notes from the prior servicer. I told her that what she had asked for, a deed in lieu with a deficiency waiver, was something we could do, and that the conditions on our side were a clean and timely turnover of the property in good broom-swept condition by a date we would agree on. She was so relieved that she cried on the phone. She honored the deal exactly. The property came back to us in good shape, on time, without the cost of a contested foreclosure, and we monetized the asset through a sale. Our investors made a meaningful return on a note that the prior lender had treated as a fight to win rather than a problem to solve.

None of that outcome was available through the prior lender. They had the same collection notes. They had the same borrower. They had the same property. What they did not have was a willingness to read the file and use the information in it to structure a solution that worked. For a note investor, the collection notes are the cheat sheet you get for free. Read them. Understand them. Use them. The borrower who has already told a prior servicer what they want is a borrower whose deal is half done before you ever pick up the phone.

The same logic applies to the rest of the servicer's file. The payment history, the late notice copies, the modification offers made and refused, any bankruptcy notices, any hardship letters submitted, and the tax and insurance escrow records all tell part of the story of the loan. The note buyer who reads that story buys a different asset than the note buyer who reads only the original loan documents.

Common Documentation Failures

To close the chapter, here are the most common documentation failures I have seen in private lending files over the years. Every one of them has been the source of a real workout problem for some lender, somewhere, who thought their file was complete and discovered after the fact that it was not.

The first common failure I see is signatures by parties who lack the authority to bind. The note or mortgage gets signed by an officer or member of an entity who did not actually have authority under the entity's operating agreement or bylaws to sign on behalf of the entity. The borrower later argues the loan does not bind the entity. A current entity authority document in the file, signed by all parties who have the right to authorize the borrowing, prevents this argument.

Improper notarization is the second common failure. The notary did not actually witness the signature, did not verify the signer's identity, did not complete the notarial certificate correctly, or used the wrong notarial form for the type of document. Notarization defects can render a document unenforceable in some jurisdictions and can certainly slow down a foreclosure.

Missing recordings cause recurring workout problems. The mortgage was executed but never recorded, or the assignment was executed but never recorded, or the deed of trust was executed but recorded in the wrong county or with the wrong legal description. Recording failures break your ability to assert priority against third parties.

Gaps in the assignment chain are another high-frequency failure. The mortgage went from Lender A to Lender B to Lender C, but only the A-to-B assignment was recorded. The B-to-C assignment is sitting in someone's file unrecorded. The public record shows B still owns the mortgage. You are C. This is a fixable problem, sometimes, if everyone involved is still in business and willing to cooperate. It is a much worse problem if any of them are not.

Allonges not properly attached to the underlying note create their own enforcement risk. The endorsement chain on the note runs out of room, an allonge is prepared with the additional endorsement, but the allonge is never physically attached to the original note. The seller hands you a note and a separate piece of paper. Some courts will accept that. Others will not. The conservative path is to insist on a properly attached allonge before you close.

Missing ISAOA language on the insurance policy is a quiet but expensive failure. The hazard policy names the originator but not its successors and assigns. You bought the note. The collateral suffers a loss. The check goes to the originator, not to you. You are now in a recovery fight with a counterparty you did not choose.

Missing builder's risk during construction is the construction-specific failure that surfaces only after something has already gone wrong on site. The construction file did not have builder's risk coverage in force at the start of the project, or the coverage lapsed mid-project, or the coverage did not carry the proper ISAOA language. The project burns down. The lender is unprotected on collateral that is largely under construction and not eligible for a standard hazard policy.

None of these failures are surprising. All of them are avoidable. A competent attorney preparing the document set, a disciplined closing checklist, a servicer or in-house team that monitors the file over its life, and a due diligence process at acquisition that confirms each of these items will catch almost every one of these failures before they become workout problems. The file you build correctly at the front end is the file that will hold up at the back end when it has to.

Dougie Downer

The document you decided not to require is the one your attorney will ask for in the first five minutes of the workout. The recording you did not pull after closing is the one that turns out to have the wrong legal description. The collection note you did not read at acquisition is the one that would have told you the borrower already offered a clean way out. Dot your i's, cross your t's, monitor what needs monitoring, and read what is in the file. Your future self will thank you.

Chapter 11

What You Need to Make It to Closing

A few years back we had a client purchase a home appraised at three hundred and fifty thousand dollars for twelve thousand dollars at the foreclosure auction. They could not believe their luck.

What they did not realize was that the judgment that had sent the property to foreclosure was the HOA lien. The first mortgage was still in force on the home, the balance on the first mortgage exceeded what the property was worth, and the first mortgage foreclosure was only weeks away. They had paid twelve thousand dollars for a position that was about to be wiped out.

A simple review of the county clerk records, or a call to the title company before a quick review, would have prevented the loss. The information was in the public record. The gap between the deal you think you bought and the deal you actually bought is what this chapter is about.

Closing day is when your capital leaves your account. It is also where fraud often shows up, and where weak operational discipline at the lender's end becomes the borrower's leverage later. The due diligence you do getting to closing, and the verifications you do leading up to it, determine whether the loan or note you underwrote and closed on actually carries the position you thought you were funding. This chapter is shorter than the ones around it on purpose. The discipline you need is not complicated. The mistakes, however, can be hard to recover from.

Title Due Diligence

Title work is not paperwork you push off on the closing agent and forget about. The title company is your partner in this process, but the position you end up in after closing is your responsibility. That responsibility starts with reading the title report yourself, asking questions about anything that looks unusual, and confirming that the lien position you are about to fund is the position you intended to fund.

Two patterns warrant a closer look on every file. The first is the related-party transfer. The seller acquired the property from a relative, a business partner, or an affiliated entity recently, at a price that does not reflect the current market, and is now selling to your borrower at a higher number. That pattern can be legitimate. It can also be the setup for a misrepresented purchase price, an inflated appraisal, or a quick flip designed to manufacture equity that does not exist. The second is the seller concession that does not match the contract. Concessions, credits, decorating allowances, and seller-paid repairs that show up at closing without being papered into the contract are signals worth a phone call before you wire funds.

The Title Search, the Commitment, the Policy, and the Exceptions

Title insurance is issued in stages. You receive a title commitment before closing, which is the title company's preliminary statement of what they are willing to insure and on what conditions. You receive the final title policy after closing, once the conditions in the commitment have been satisfied. Between the two is the exceptions schedule, and the exceptions schedule is where close scrutiny is required.

The exceptions schedule lists everything the title company is not insuring. Easements, restrictions, prior recorded matters, surveys not provided, mineral rights reserved, and any number of other items show up on that list. A title policy that excepts the very liens or encumbrances you are worried about is not doing what you need it to do. Read the exceptions schedule on every file. Ask the title company to remove anything that should not be there. Confirm at the final policy stage that the exceptions you negotiated out actually came out of the final policy.

The same workflow applies on note acquisitions. The title policy that protects the original lender transfers in some states automatically and in other states only with an endorsement or an assignment. Confirm the position in your jurisdiction and require whatever documentation is needed to keep the title insurance in force for your benefit.

Title Search Versus Title Opinion

A handful of states still distinguish between a title search and a title opinion. A title search is a records check performed by the title company or an abstractor. A title opinion is a legal opinion rendered by an attorney based on that search. In the states that follow the title-opinion model, the attorney's opinion carries weight that a search alone does not, and the malpractice coverage behind the opinion is part of the protection package the lender is buying. If you are lending in one of those states, know what you are getting and price the closing accordingly. Keep in mind that neither is an actual title insurance policy. The search and the opinion lead up to a policy, but they do not replace it.

Closing Protection Letters and the Closing Agent

The closing protection letter, sometimes called an insured closing letter, is a document from the title insurance underwriter confirming that they will stand behind the closing agent's handling of funds and document execution at closing. It is not the title policy itself. On any closing where the lender is wiring funds, the closing protection letter belongs in the file.

Wire Instruction Verification

Wire fraud at closing is the simplest fraud in this business to prevent, and the one most often allowed to happen anyway. It is not a joke. Our NMLS-licensed mortgage company closes many purchase transactions for consumers, and every title company and closing attorney we work with carries a wire fraud disclaimer in their email signature. There is a specific procedure for confirming that wire instructions are correct, and that procedure exists because email accounts get hacked all the time. Criminals have become very adept at pretending to be people they are not. The most common scam, the one that works rarely but produces a windfall for the criminal when it does, is an email sent to the borrower pretending to be the closing agent, asking the borrower to wire their funds to closing using new wiring information. The information sends the money to the criminal's account. Not too long ago, a title company handling one of our clients' closings was hacked. The borrower received the fraudulent wire request and did not call the title company to confirm. He wired his money. He lost all of it, and the closing never happened. The fix is simple. Treat every wire instruction you receive by email as suspect. Call the title company or the closing attorney at the number on their website, or on a prior closing statement, and verbally confirm the wire instructions before any funds move. Never call the number on the email. The criminal who sent the email also controlled that number.

Closing-Day Verifications

The closing day itself is the last chance you have for verifications before funding. Confirm the insurance binder is in place with the lender named correctly on the mortgagee clause. Confirm the borrower has paid the first premium or that funds for the premium are accounted for in the closing statement. Confirm the final walk-through of the property has been completed where the loan documents require it and the condition of the property has not changed since the appraisal. Confirm signing authority for any entity borrower.

Two stories from my own career illustrate why these small confirmations are important.

A number of years ago, two siblings and an older father came to us for a loan. We approved the loan and were working toward closing. As the closing date approached, the father could not make the closing. There was always an excuse as to why he could not be reached. The pattern got our attention. Further due diligence uncovered that the father was in an assisted living facility and suffered from Alzheimer's. He was not competent to sign. The two siblings, who were the other guarantors on the loan, had been hiding that fact. The father was the financial strength on the file. Without him, it was a different loan than the one we had approved, and the signature we had been asked to take would not have been valid even if we had taken it.

A longer time ago, a borrower arrived at closing with a woman who was not his wife. Something about her identification did not look right. It turned out the woman was the borrower's girlfriend, who resembled the borrower's wife and was carrying the wife's identification. The actual wife knew nothing about the property the husband was buying.

You have to watch your deals like a hawk because you will be surprised how many times people will try to slide things past you. The borrower who arrives with the wrong person, or who arranges for someone else to sign in their place, or who has brought a relative whose competence to bind themselves is in question, has decided that the lender's verification is the only thing standing between the fraud and the funded loan. Sometimes they are right.

Construction Closings

Construction closings have their own additional layer. The initial funding does not represent the full loan. It funds the acquisition and whatever portion of the budget the borrower needs up front. The remaining budget will move through draws over the life of the project. The lender at the initial closing has to set up the draw process according to the agreed-upon draw schedule.

A construction closing should include a budget review against the contractor's scope of work, qualification of the general contractor (license, insurance, references, capacity to handle the project), confirmation of the builder's risk insurance with the lender properly named on the mortgagee clause, and the documentation of the first draw and each subsequent draw as they come. The first draw is often funded at or near closing to cover initial site work or materials. Treat it as the first test of the draw process. If the lien waivers, the inspection report, and the supporting documentation are not in order at the first draw, you'll need to tighten up that process before you release additional draws as the project moves forward.

Note Acquisitions

Your due diligence on a note acquisition follows a similar thought process. Before the funds leave your account, confirm the endorsement chain on the original promissory note is intact. Confirm the recorded assignments of the mortgage or deed of trust close the gap from the original lender to the seller you are buying from. Confirm the servicing transfer file is in place and that the records the new servicer will need to start collection in the first month after closing are accounted for. Confirm the seller has the authority to convey the loan to you, and that whatever consents or board approvals their structure requires have been obtained.

Anti-Money Laundering and Source of Funds

Anti-Money Laundering (AML) compliance is part of the closing process whether or not the lender is a federally regulated institution. Federal law assigns responsibility for monitoring and reporting suspicious activity to financial institutions and to certain non-bank financial professionals, and private lenders, title companies, and settlement agents all operate inside that framework to varying degrees. The detail of who is required to do what under the Bank Secrecy Act and related regulations is a question for your counsel. The operational reality at the closing table is the same in every case.

The most visible piece of AML work at closing is the source of funds requirement. The lender, the title company, and the closing agent all need to be able to document where the borrower's cash to close came from. Wires from titled accounts at known financial institutions are great, but how did the borrower come into possession of the money in the first place? You usually want to go back 60-90 days to "source" those deposits. Regulators are usually looking to ensure that you've checked that the money isn't being laundered in some shape or form. Cashier's checks supported by bank statements showing the funds were on deposit for a reasonable period before closing are usually acceptable. Cash that the borrower walks in with, without supporting documentation, is not clean and should not be accepted. The reason is straightforward. The lender, the title company, and the closing agent are not permitted to launder funds, knowingly or unknowingly, through a real estate transaction. The borrower who shows up with a substantial amount of cash that has no documented source has presented a problem that no closing professional can solve in the moment. That is also why neither the lender nor the title company can accept cash kept under the mattress, no matter how reasonable the borrower's explanation sounds.

A clean closing from an AML standpoint looks like this. The borrower's cash to close arrives from titled bank accounts, with documentation showing the funds were not deposited in a lump sum the week before closing. Any large recent deposits in the borrower's account history are explained and supported. The settlement statement reflects every dollar coming in and every dollar going out, with no off-ledger payments. The lender's file documents the review of the source of funds, the questions that were asked, and the answers that were received. If the file is ever reviewed down the road, the documentation will support what the closing statement reflects.

A note investor at acquisition is buying a file that was originated under someone else's AML procedures. The due diligence work includes confirming that the originator's source-of-funds documentation is in the file and is consistent with the closing statement.

Dougie Downer

You expect what you inspect, and title is no exception. Develop a great relationship with your local title company. Make sure you're thoroughly inspecting the title reports to ensure you're in the lien position you think you are. Mechanic's liens, HOA liens, and other clouds on the title tend to sneak up on investors, costing them their hard-earned capital.

Chapter 12

The Credit Memo, the Loan Officer Memorandum, and the Underwriting File

My loan officers and processors think I am off my rocker. In my commercial lending days, we prepared a written analysis on every loan we did, and I titled mine the Loan Officer Memorandum. It went into the file that was presented to the underwriter, and it explained the borrower, the property, the program, the numbers, and my line of thinking on every part of the file that the underwriter was likely to question. I have carried that practice into consumer lending, where almost nobody else does it. Loan officers in the consumer space roll their eyes when I describe it. They are taught that the application, the credit report, the income documents, and the bank statements are enough on their own. In a clean file maybe that's true. In a file with any complexity at all, it is not, and the deal is better served when the loan officer says so out loud, on paper, before the underwriter has to figure it out alone.

Chapter 11 covered what happens at and through closing, when capital leaves your account and your lien position is recorded. This chapter goes the other direction. It covers the document trail that explains why the loan was and should be approved in the first place, what conditions were imposed at each stage, and what exceptions were granted along the way. A working credit officer writes a memo on every transaction. The private lender or note investor who funds a loan or acquires a note without a memo behind it is winging it, and you miss things when you wing it.

One important note before we go any further. Most mortgage loan officers and most private lenders never use a Loan Officer Memorandum at all when submitting a loan. I am the weirdo. I find that the discipline of writing it helps me be thorough as I prepare the file, and the LOM is crucial to presenting a great package to whoever is going to approve it. If you take nothing else from this chapter, take that.

Three Documents, Three Different Jobs

Three documents tend to get lumped together under the heading of "credit memo," and they do three different jobs. The Loan Officer Memorandum is the document the loan officer prepares to present the loan package to the underwriter. In it, the loan officer walks through the borrower, the property, the program, and the deal. The loan officer also anticipates the underwriter's questions and answers them in advance. The Credit Memo, sometimes called the Conditional Approval, is the document the underwriter sends back. It is the checklist of conditions the underwriter is imposing before the loan can move to docs, to funding, and after closing. The Underwriting File is the assembled package of everything else. The application, the credit report, the income documents, the bank statements, the appraisal, the title commitment, the entity documents, the insurance binders, and every other piece of supporting documentation the underwriter needed to reach a decision.

In a traditional bank, these three documents are prepared by three different sets of hands. The loan officer prepares the LOM, the underwriter responds with the Credit Memo, and the processor assembles the underwriting file. In private lending, where one person often wears all three hats, the practice of separating these documents in your own mind is what keeps the file from collapsing into a stack of paper with no explanation behind it. The LOM is your line of thinking. The Credit Memo is the conditions you are imposing on yourself or on the loan you are presenting to someone else. The underwriting file is the evidence.

What Belongs in a Loan Officer Memorandum

A complete LOM walks through the loan from top to bottom. It opens with a borrower and entity description. Who is the borrower. If the borrower is an entity, what is the entity, who owns it, who controls it, and what is the entity authorized to do. It identifies the guarantors and their relationship to the borrower. It establishes that you know who you are lending to.

It then provides a transaction summary. What is the loan amount. What is being purchased or refinanced. What is the purpose of the loan. What is the structure. What is the source and use of funds at closing. A reader who knows nothing about the deal should be able to read the transaction summary and understand the basic shape of what is being financed.

It describes the program. What product is the borrower being approved under. What are the rate, the term, the amortization, the prepayment terms, and any other material economic terms. If the program has eligibility requirements, the LOM confirms the borrower meets them, and if the borrower misses one, it flags the exception and explains the offset.

It walks through the Three C's. Character, Capacity, and Collateral. We covered each one in its own chapter earlier in the book, so the LOM is where you bring them together for this specific deal. Character covers the borrower's credit history, payment history, public records, and reputation, and explains any items on the credit report that warrant a comment. Capacity covers the borrower's ability to repay from the sources of repayment identified in the file, with the income analysis tied back to the supporting documents. Collateral covers the property itself, the appraised value, the lien position, the loan-to-value, any title issues, and the borrower's equity contribution.

It identifies the sources of repayment. The primary source is what the borrower is going to pay you back with under normal operating conditions. The secondary source is what you collect against if the primary source fails. On a rental property, the primary source might be the rental income and the secondary source the sale or refinance of the property. On a fix-and-flip, the primary source is the sale of the rehabbed property and the secondary source is the borrower's other liquidity or the lender's ability to take and finish the project. The LOM names the sources explicitly so there is no ambiguity later about what the deal was supposed to do.

It documents exceptions to policy. Every lender has a set of guidelines, and every guideline gets bent from time to time for the right deal. The LOM is where the loan officer identifies what is being asked outside of policy, why the file supports the exception, and what compensating factors justify the request. An exception that is documented up front and approved on its own merits is a different file than an exception that gets discovered three months into servicing because nobody wrote it down.

It closes with whatever additional context the file needs. That context can include the borrower's background, the sponsor's experience, prior deals with the same borrower, market context for the collateral, and any other detail that helps the reader understand what is being approved. The LOM is not a form. It is the loan officer's narrative, and the narrative should be as long as the deal requires.

The LOM as a Living Document

My LOM starts as a Word template. The headers are already there. Overview, Borrower, Subject Property, Income, Assets, Credit, Program, Sources of Repayment, Exceptions, and a few more depending on the deal. You can add your own headings to match how you operate. The point of the template is to keep me from forgetting a section, not to lock me into a fixed format. Once the template is open, I treat it as a living document. I add to it as I work through the file. As I review the credit report, the income documents, the bank statements, and the appraisal, I write into the corresponding section while what I am seeing is fresh.

Two sections at the bottom of my template have done more for the quality of my files than almost anything else I do. The first is a section I title "Questions for Borrower." As I work through the file and items come up that I need to ask the customer, I write the question out, in plain language, as if I were typing it into an email to the borrower. That way, I don't see a squirrel outside, get distracted, and forget to ask the question. I bullet them as they come. When I have worked through everything and the questions are all in place, I copy the list, paste it into a single email, and send it. Customers hate it when you keep coming back nickel and diming them with one question at a time. They appreciate it when you knock the questions out at once.

The second section I title "Salient Points." These are not questions for the borrower. They are notes to myself, the underwriter, and the processor about things in the file that I need to keep in mind. Mr. Jones will be out of the country and unavailable until July 15. The property had a new roof installed in June of 2025. Lawrence prefers to go by Larry. None of these items are deal points by themselves, and none of them belong in an email to the borrower, but I want them in front of me as I work the file.

The result of building the LOM this way is that by the time the file is ready to submit, I have done most of the thinking up front. The story is written. The exceptions are documented. The questions have been asked and answered. The notes on the borrower's situation are in one place. The underwriter receives a package that does not need me on the phone to walk them through it, and the loan officer who built it knows the file in a way that someone who skipped this step never will.

The Credit Memo, also known as the Conditional Approval

The Credit Memo is the underwriter's response to the package. In consumer lending it is most often called the Conditional Approval. The underwriter has reviewed the file, reached a decision, and listed the conditions that have to be cleared before the loan can move to docs, to funding, and on to post-closing. Each condition is assigned to a stage in the workflow, and each stage has its own place.

"Prior To Documents," sometimes shortened to PTD, are the conditions that have to be cleared before the closing documents are drawn. These are the items that affect what the documents say, and they include the final entity authority, the final loan amount, the final program, the final terms, and the identification of the final guarantors. If a PTD condition is unresolved, the documents cannot be drawn correctly, and drawing them anyway and trying to fix the file later is how loans close on the wrong terms.

"Prior To Funding," sometimes shortened to PTF, are the conditions that have to be cleared before the lender wires money. These are the items that confirm the closing is actually ready to happen, and they include final title clearance, insurance binders with the correct mortgagee clause, updated payoff figures on the refinance side, confirmation that the conditions on the closing protection letter have been met, and verbal verification of the wire instructions. PTF conditions are the lender's last line of defense before the money leaves the account.

"Post-Closing Conditions" are the items that have to be received after funding to complete the file, and they include the recorded mortgage or deed of trust, the final title policy, the original signed note with the proper endorsements, and the recorded assignments where applicable. A file with open post-closing conditions thirty, sixty, or ninety days after funding is a file that is going to surface a problem at the worst possible time, usually when the loan is being sold to a secondary buyer or pulled into a workout. Clearing post-closing conditions on a defined timeline is part of the process of running a credit operation rather than just funding loans.

One point that catches new lenders by surprise is that providing the document the underwriter asked for is not the same thing as clearing the condition. The bank statements come in with a large unexplained deposit. That large deposit becomes another condition to clear. The tax return arrives with a business the borrower never mentioned on the application. That becomes yet another condition to be addressed. The appraisal comes back at a value below the purchase price. The structure of the loan has to be rebuilt around the new value. The Credit Memo is not a static checklist. The conditions evolve as the documents come in, and the loan officer who treats the original list as the finish line is going to be surprised when the underwriter keeps adding to it as new concerns surface.

Exceptions to Policy

Every good lender operates from a written set of guidelines, and every set of guidelines gets bent from time to time when appropriate. The exception to policy is the formal acknowledgment that the file does not meet a stated guideline, the documented reasoning for granting the exception, and the compensating factors that justify the decision. A file approved on an exception, with the exception documented in the LOM, in the Credit Memo, and in the loan file, is defensible. A file approved on an exception that nobody wrote down is a problem waiting to happen.

The compensating factors are facts that support the exception. A borrower whose debt-to-income ratio sits 2 points above policy might be approved on an exception if liquidity, reserves, payment history, and collateral position more than offset the ratio. A borrower whose loan-to-value sits a few points above policy might be approved on an exception if the borrower brings additional collateral, a stronger guaranty, or a shorter term. Document the factors. Tie them to the file. Approve on the merits, not on your gut.

The exception is also where private lenders most often get themselves into trouble. The borrower is a friend of a friend. The relationship is good. The borrower is a "nice guy." The guideline gets bent without anyone writing down why, and the file moves forward as if the guideline never existed. Then the loan goes sideways, the lender sits down with the file, and there is nothing on paper explaining why the guideline was waived. The defensible exception is the documented exception. The undocumented exception is the file you do not want to be holding when someone asks you to explain it.

One other reason you do not want to approve policy exceptions without a very good reason is the appearance of discrimination. You have to be consistent with your decision making. If you were to ever get sued for discriminatory underwriting, even if there was no discriminatory intent, attorneys are going to dig into your files looking for ways to twist things to their benefit. Let's say they find two similar files. One is a file you approved with an exception, and the other is their client's file that you declined on a similar fact pattern. If you did not document your thoughts on the exception, you might be in trouble. You must protect your practice and portfolio.

Who Uses the Memo, and When

The LOM and the Credit Memo are not documents you write once and file away. They are working documents that get used across the life of the loan. The underwriter uses them at approval to understand the deal and to set conditions. The processor uses them through closing to make sure each condition is being addressed. The servicer uses them through the life of the loan to understand the borrower, the collateral, the sources of repayment, and the exceptions that were granted. If the loan goes sideways and a workout attorney picks up the file, the memo is what gives the attorney the reasons the loan was approved in the first place, what the borrower's situation looked like at origination, and where the original lender drew the lines. If a regulator or an examiner ever asks to see the file, the memo gives them their first answers before they get to their second questions.

Without a memo in the file, every one of those readers has to reconstruct the deal from the raw documents. Some of them will get it right. Some of them will get it wrong. The short time the loan officer spent writing the LOM at origination saves dozens of hours of confusion downstream, and it keeps the story of the loan consistent through every hand the file passes through.

Scaling the Memo to a Private Lender's Operation

A private lender or note investor does not need to replicate the format of a bank credit package to get the benefit of this process. The point is not the form. The point is the line of thinking that occurred. A one-page memo on a clean single-asset deal is enough if the page actually addresses the borrower, the collateral, the program, the sources of repayment, the Three C's, and any exceptions. A longer memo on a complex deal with multiple guarantors, layered collateral, or construction draws is appropriate when the file warrants it. Match the depth of the memo to the depth of the deal.

What you do not want is a template that gets filled out the same way every time regardless of the file. The form-filling exercise produces a memo that says the right things in the right boxes without giving the underwriter and the servicer anything they did not already know. The memo has to be written. It does not have to be long. It has to actually engage with what is unusual or interesting about the deal in front of you.

The private lender who builds this habit on the first few loans they fund will fund the rest with far more discipline than the lender who never uses it. The note investor who writes a short memo on every purchase will buy a stronger portfolio than the investor who buys on price and gut feel. The memo is the evidence that the deal was actually underwritten well.

The Memo at Note Acquisition

On a note purchase, the memo is not the original loan officer's write-up. The original loan officer is gone, and you may or may not even see what they wrote at origination. The memo at acquisition is your own due diligence write-up supporting the purchase decision. It walks through the same elements the original LOM should have walked through, but it is written from the buyer's perspective on the loan as it exists today rather than on the loan as it was made.

At acquisition, the memo identifies the borrower as they are today, not as they were at origination. The borrower may have divorced, moved, changed business structures, or stopped paying. It identifies the collateral as it exists today. The property may have appreciated, depreciated, suffered damage, been improved, or changed use. It identifies the current status of the loan, whether the loan is performing, sub-performing, in default, in forbearance, in litigation, or in foreclosure. It identifies the sources of repayment available today. The borrower may have lost the income stream the original loan was approved against, or the property may now be the only practical source of repayment. It documents the condition of the file, the chain of assignments, the endorsement chain on the note, the recorded mortgage, the title policy, the insurance, and any defects discovered in due diligence. It documents the exceptions you are accepting as part of the purchase, the price you are paying, and the reasons the file supports the bid.

A note investor who writes this memo on every purchase builds a portfolio that can be defended at any point in its life cycle. A note investor who skips this step buys a stack of files, hopes the loans perform, and reacts to problems as they surface. The first investor is running a credit operation. The second is collecting paper and praying.

Documents Provided Does Not Mean File Is Ready

One last point worth making. A loan officer who has gathered every document the underwriter requested has not necessarily produced a file that is ready to close. Each new document raises as many questions as it answers. There is a deposit on the bank statement that needs explanation. There is a business on the tax return that has to be added to the analysis. There is a condition issue in the appraisal that affects the loan amount. There is an exception on the title commitment that has to be cleared. Each new document can spark another condition, and the file is not ready until the questions stop and the conditions are clear.

That is also the answer to the loan officer who tells the borrower their file is ready when the borrower delivered the last requested item. It is not ready. It is ready for the underwriter to look at again, and the underwriter may have another round of questions before it is actually ready. The key is to manage the borrower's expectations directly. Each round of documents brings the file closer to ready. The file is ready when the underwriter says it is ready, not when the borrower delivers the last document on the most recent list.

Dougie Downer

Most loan officers wing it when they submit a file to underwriting. The best loan officers take the time up front to ask themselves what reasons the underwriter might find to turn the file down, and what a good underwriter is going to ask for. The good loan officer gathers that documentation up front so the process does not slow down later. The lazy loan officer waits to be told. Be the good loan officer.

Chapter 13

Servicing the Loan After the Closing

On my first note buy, I was stupid. I signed a servicing agreement with a clause that I missed at the time. For the monthly fee I was paying per file, the servicer would perform three collection actions on a delinquent loan. That sounded reasonable enough when I read it. What I found out later was that, to this particular servicer, a collection action was dialing the borrower's phone number, hearing that the number was disconnected, and recording the result. Three of those dials equaled the three collection actions promised in the contract. The bill kept arriving and the loan kept getting older, and the servicer had technically delivered exactly what the agreement called for. That was a rough lesson on a contract I had not read carefully enough, and it was where my respect for monitoring my servicer began.

Closing is only the start of the loan, not the end of it. The money leaves your account, the security instrument gets recorded, the file is bundled up, and at exactly that moment the operational function of servicing begins. Servicing is the steady, often invisible work that keeps the loan performing as approved, keeps the records straight, and keeps the lender or note holder in a defensible position when something changes. A loan that is not properly serviced is a loan that is slowly becoming unsecured. For the note investor, the servicing transfer at acquisition is where much of the value documented in the file can be lost if the documentation and the boarding process are not handled correctly.

Use a Licensed Third-Party Servicer

My strong recommendation, on most loans, in most states, for most private lenders and note investors, is to outsource servicing to a licensed third-party servicer. In many cases the recommendation is moot because the law requires it. Loans secured by owner-occupied residential property are the clearest example. Servicing those loans without the appropriate state licenses, registrations, and regulatory disclosures is not a corner private lenders should be trying to cut. Investor-purpose and commercial loans give the lender a little more flexibility, but flexibility is not the same as competence, and the practical question on every loan should be whether the in-house team has the expertise, the systems, and the time to do this work to a professional standard month after month.

In-house servicing looks cheap until the first borrower stops paying, the first insurance policy lapses, the first property tax bill goes unpaid, or the first borrower files for bankruptcy. At that moment the lender discovers what a professional servicer actually does, and the cost of doing it badly suddenly exceeds the cost of having it done correctly from the start. A licensed servicer carries the state authorizations, the system of record, the call recording, the cash management, the disclosure machinery, and the staff who actually know what to do when something changes. A small private lender trying to replicate any one of those components in-house is taking on a job that gets harder, not easier, as the portfolio grows.

There are a few situations in which in-house servicing makes sense. A very small portfolio of business purpose loans to repeat borrowers the lender knows personally, where the lender has the time and the recordkeeping habits to handle it, can work. A family office with its own credit, licensing, and operations team can run an internal servicing function. Most private lenders are not in that situation. Most private lenders should be paying a professional servicer to do this function and spending their own time on origination, credit, and portfolio decisions, where they actually add the most value.

What Servicing Actually Does

At the most basic level, servicing collects the payment, applies the cash to the right buckets in the right order, and keeps the ledger. That sounds simple. It is not. The payment intake has to be timely. The cash application has to follow the order set in the note: late charges, default interest, regular interest, principal, escrow, and any other agreed sequence. The ledger has to balance to the penny month over month, with every receipt and every disbursement traceable to a source document. A ledger that drifts by even a few dollars over time becomes a ledger you cannot use to demonstrate the balance in a courtroom, and the borrower whose payoff figure you are trying to defend will find every cent that you cannot account for.

Beyond the payment and the ledger, the servicer issues monthly statements, year-end statements, and the IRS information returns that apply to the loan type and the lender. Form 1098 reporting on mortgage interest, Form 1099 reporting where the structure requires it, and any state-level reporting are all the servicer's role on a properly outsourced file. The records of every payment, every late notice, every borrower conversation, and every change to the loan are kept in the system of record where they can be retrieved years later. A creditor rights attorney picking up the file two years after a default needs the complete payment history, the complete communication log, and the complete record of every notice that went out. A servicer that has been doing their job correctly delivers all of it on request. A servicer that has not is the reason the workout costs more than it should.

Escrow and Impound Accounts on Investor and Commercial Loans

Escrow and impound accounts for property taxes and hazard insurance are standard on owner-occupied residential loans and optional on most investor and commercial loans. The optional part is the trap. A private lender who decides not to escrow on an investor loan is trusting the borrower to pay the property taxes when they come due and to keep the insurance current month after month. Some borrowers do. Many do not, especially when cash gets tight. The first time the lender discovers that the taxes are delinquent is often the first time the lender discovers that a tax lien now sits ahead of their first mortgage, and the first time the lender finds out the hazard policy lapsed is sometimes the day the property burns.

Requiring an escrow on investor and commercial loans takes those scenarios off the table. The borrower pays one combined monthly amount, the servicer holds the tax and insurance portions in the escrow account, and the bills get paid on time from a source the lender controls. The administrative cost is modest. The protection is meaningful. On any loan where the lender has the option to require escrow and the credit reason to want one, the right answer is to require it and to have the servicer administer it the way they would on a regulated residential loan.

Insurance and Tax Monitoring as a Continuing Function

Chapter 10 Parts 1 and 2 covered the insurance protocol at origination and through the life of the loan, including the mortgagee clause language, the ISAOA and ATIMA endorsements, the builder's risk requirement on construction collateral, and the force-placed coverage process when a borrower's policy lapses. The servicer enforces that protocol through the life of the loan. The servicer receives renewal certificates, confirms that coverage continues at the right amount with the right mortgagee clause, flags any policy that does not renew or that renews with reduced coverage, and triggers force-placed coverage when the borrower fails to replace a lapsed policy. The same logic applies to property taxes at the parcel level. The servicer monitors for delinquencies, notifies the lender of any problem, and on escrowed loans pays the bills directly out of the escrow account. A private lender trying to run this function in-house, across a portfolio of any size, is signing up for a job that is much larger and much more time-sensitive than it looks from the outside.

Borrower Communication and Recordkeeping

Every conversation with the borrower gets recorded in the servicing system. Every late notice, every demand, every modification discussion, every promise to pay, every email, every voicemail, and every in-person meeting belongs in the log. The reason is the same reason the ledger has to balance to the penny. Years later, in a workout, a foreclosure, or bankruptcy proceeding, someone is going to ask what the borrower said in month seventeen and what the lender said in response. The answer needs to come from the file, not from anyone's recollection. A professional servicer treats this recordkeeping as a baseline function. An in-house operation must build this on its own, and most do not think of it until something goes wrong and the records are not there.

Read the Servicing Agreement Carefully

Choosing a servicer is a credit decision in itself. The basic monthly fee per file covers the standard servicing work, which is sending statements, collecting payments, posting to the ledger, and handling the routine borrower communication on a performing loan. Beyond that, every servicer maintains an a la carte menu of additional services that get billed separately. Handling a bankruptcy filing, negotiating a reaffirmation, processing a modification, ordering a broker price opinion, coordinating with foreclosure counsel, managing force-placed insurance, handling a loss claim, and managing an REO file are all line items with their own pricing. The fees vary widely across the industry, and on a file that runs into trouble, the a la carte items add up fast.

I learned this early in my portfolio management career. On one of my files, a servicer attempted to earn a substantial lump sum fee for negotiating updated payment arrangements with a delinquent borrower. The structure of that fee gave the servicer a real incentive to put any troubled loan on a modified payment plan whether the circumstances supported one or not. The principle that should govern that decision is the question of whether the borrower's problem is temporary or permanent. A temporary problem (a job change, a medical event, a one-time business interruption) can sometimes be addressed by a structured retasking of the payment terms. A permanent problem (a borrower whose underlying income or business cannot support the loan as written) cannot. Putting a borrower with a permanent problem onto a retasked payment plan does nothing but delay the loss, generate fees for the servicer, and let the lender pretend the loan is still performing. Re-defaults on those files are common, and when they happen, the servicer earns the retasking fee again.

Knowing all of that, I had a clause in my servicing agreement that required my final approval on any retasking of a loan. The clause was clear. The servicer signed it. On that one file, that servicer negotiated updated payment terms with the borrower and signed a written agreement without ever bringing the proposal to me for approval. The fee triggered. The retasking went through. I found out after the fact. That was an expensive lesson on two fronts. The first was that some servicers will quietly do what generates their fee and ask forgiveness later if asked at all. The second was that the servicer fought me tooth and nail before refunding the bogus fee, and the borrower could not perform on the unauthorized modification, which dragged the workout out even longer. You cannot assume the servicer is acting in your interest or in the borrower's interest. Many times the servicer is acting in the servicer's interest, and the agreement you signed is the only place you have any leverage to push back.

When you choose a servicer, read every line of the agreement. Understand what is included in the base fee and what gets billed separately. Understand the fee structure on every a la carte item, especially the items that the servicer has an incentive to perform whether they are appropriate or not. Insist on written notice and prior approval clauses on the decisions that should remain with the lender, including any modification, any retasking, any forbearance, any short payoff, and any deed in lieu...and then audit often. A clause is only as good as the audit behind it.

Stay on Your Timelines

Servicers and the foreclosure attorneys they work with will, if left to their own pace, take their own sweet time moving a file forward. This is not a knock on any individual firm. It is the nature of the business. They have a hundred other files in front of yours, and the loan that is not getting attention from the lender tends to be the loan that does not get attention from anyone. Every state has statutory notice periods built into the foreclosure process. Missouri's power-of-sale process, as one example, runs on specific notice timelines. When the thirty-day notice goes out, the next action should be moving forward on day thirty-one, not on day sixty, and not when the file rotates back to the top of someone's desk. It needs to be moving on day thirty-one.

For that reason, on every file that moves into default, I insist on direct selection of the foreclosure attorney and direct communication with that attorney throughout the process. The servicer may have a preferred panel of foreclosure firms, and there is sometimes nothing wrong with using a firm from that panel if the firm is competent and the rates are reasonable. Usually, however, they are foreclosure mills and they do a poor job of handling a file. What is not acceptable is allowing the servicer to manage the relationship and to relay information from the attorney to me on the servicer's schedule. The lender who wants the foreclosure moving in a timely manner needs to be talking directly to the lawyer who is filing the paperwork. Be the squeaky wheel. If a servicer won't allow this, find another servicer. They work for you...not the other way around. The carrying cost of a stalled foreclosure is real money, and every month that the file sits is a month of default interest, taxes, insurance, and legal fees the lender may or may not recover. Watch the timelines. Push when pushing is required. Choose firms that respond to that pressure rather than firms that resent it.

The Servicing Transfer at Note Acquisition

When a note is purchased, the loan has to move from the seller's servicer to the buyer's servicer. This transfer is called boarding. The records and documents that move with the loan include the payment history, the cash application detail, the communication log, the late notices, the modification history, the escrow ledger, the insurance and tax records, the borrower contact information, and copies of every notice that has been sent. The records that often do not move automatically include the original note with its endorsement chain, the original recorded mortgage and any assignments, the original title policy, and the closing file. Those original instruments have to be requested, tracked, and confirmed received.

In the first thirty days after acquisition, the new servicer has to set up the loan on its system, confirm the next payment due date, confirm the escrow balance, confirm the insurance coverage is current with the correct mortgagee clause, confirm property taxes are current, send the welcome letter to the borrower with the new payment address, and document any gaps in the file that have to be filled. Federal law requires specific borrower notifications on a servicing transfer of regulated loans, and even on business purpose loans where the federal notice rules do not directly apply, a written notification to the borrower at the moment of transfer is good practice. Without it, the borrower keeps mailing payments to the old servicer, the old servicer eventually forwards them or does not, and the new file looks delinquent on its first day.

The cleaner the boarding, the better the loan performs out of the gate. The messier the boarding, the more time the new lender spends fixing problems that should not have existed in the first place. Treat the servicing transfer with the same care you would give to the closing itself, because operationally it is the closing of the acquisition.

Dougie Downer

Choosing the right servicer and watching them closely can move the needle on your portfolio returns more than most lenders ever realize. A servicer who milks the bill, or a foreclosure attorney who takes their sweet time, quietly robs you of return on every file they touch. Expect what you inspect. Watch your servicing and your legal teams like a hawk.

Part Four

When Things Go Sideways

Part Four covers the loans that go wrong. Some loans stop paying because the borrower lost a job. Some stop paying because the deal was bad from the start. Either way, the lender ends up working through a default, a workout, or a foreclosure. The chapters that follow walk through what to do at each step.

By the end of Part Four the reader should know how to spot trouble early, how to work it out cleanly, and how to recover what is recoverable when the workout fails.

Chapter 14

Monitoring the Live Loan

Several years ago, on a swing through St. Louis to inspect the collateral on a portfolio we had recently acquired, I pulled up to one of our addresses and found a nice grassy lot where the house was supposed to be. I looked at the address. I looked at the file. I looked at the grassy lot again. The recent broker price opinion in the file, prepared by a local agent, showed a cute little home sitting on that lot. The portfolio itself was a mess. We had taken on a large block of lower-end non-performing loans from a seller I had met at a conference, and the files were poorly kept when we received them. Nay, they were a complete wreck. I had been hoping the actual collateral on those loans would look better than the files made it look. The reality was worse. A neighbor was mowing the next yard over, so I walked across the lot to ask. "Sir, what happened to the house that used to be here?" "Oh, that burned down years ago." The agent who prepared the BPO had pulled an old photograph from the MLS and had obviously never set foot on the property. That is not a BPO. That is a lazy agent who didn't think we would pay attention.

That property visit is the entire chapter in one paragraph. Servicing keeps the loan running on its terms. Monitoring is the separate credit function of watching the loan, the collateral, and the borrower for early signals that the file is moving away from how it was approved, and watching the servicer and other vendors to make sure they are doing their jobs. Most defaults are recognizable long before the first missed payment for the lender or note holder who is actually looking. The lender who is not looking finds out later when the loan goes into default, and by that point the options have narrowed and the costs have grown.

Servicing Versus Monitoring

Chapter 13 covered servicing as the operational function that collects the payment, applies the cash, keeps the ledger, sends the statements, handles the IRS reporting, and tracks insurance and tax compliance through the system of record. A good servicer surfaces certain signals automatically. The borrower missed a payment. The insurance policy did not renew. The property tax bill was returned undelivered. Force-placed coverage was triggered. Those signals must be noticed, and a properly run servicing relationship will bring them to your attention on time. Servicing alone is not monitoring. Servicing reports what has already happened in the categories the servicer is contractually paid to watch. Monitoring is the lender's separate credit function of looking at the loan, the collateral, the borrower, and the portfolio with a credit officer's eye, in the categories the servicer is not paid to watch, before the signal gets large enough to become a red flag.

The two functions cannot collapse into one without losing the credit oversight. The servicer is not pricing your portfolio risk. The servicer is not evaluating whether your concentration to a particular borrower is becoming a problem. The servicer is not driving past the property to see whether the roof is still intact. The servicer is not reading between the lines of a borrower's email to notice that the tone changed recently. Those are credit officer functions, and they have to be performed by the lender or by someone the lender hires to perform them. On a small private lending operation that someone is usually the lender.

Property Visits and What They Actually Catch

Property visits are the cornerstone of collateral monitoring. A BPO is a paid opinion from someone who may or may not have driven by the property. An appraisal is a point-in-time valuation done at origination by someone who almost certainly will not return. Neither one replaces the lender's own eyes on the collateral at periodic intervals through the life of the loan. The grassy lot in St. Louis is one of the most extreme examples I have ever encountered, but in milder forms the same things show up in many portfolios. The roof that was replaced on paper and was not replaced in reality. The six-unit building listed in the file that turns out to be four units when you walk it. The "stabilized rental" that has been vacant for some time.

On a portfolio of any size, periodic visits do not require the lender to personally inspect every property every quarter. They do require a routine. On income property, I want one of our people or a paid inspector checking on the property at least once in the first year, and on a frequency keyed to the file size and the risk profile after that. On construction collateral, visits are not optional and they are not occasional. The draw inspection covered in Chapter 9 is part of this routine, and the lender or the lender's inspector should be at the property before every funded draw without exception. On REO that the lender holds for resale, visits are essential. If you are not seeing the asset, you are only being told what the contractor wants you to hear.

We had pretty good luck with a contractor out of Indianapolis on renovations to a few foreclosed properties we listed for sale. When the same contractor told us they could handle the renovation on a property in Terre Haute, we had no problem hiring them. They were going to be our boots on the ground. They farmed the actual work out to a local sub in Terre Haute, which we did not know about. I like to make surprise visits, and I do not warn people when I am about to show up. I'm based in Tampa, so the Indianapolis crew had no reason to think I would be anywhere near Indiana on short notice. As it happened, I was running an Indiana swing of asset tours that took me through Terre Haute. I had the lockbox code in the file. I stopped by the property unannounced.

The work was nowhere close to where it should have been on the timeline I was paying for. The real horror show was in the basement. Three feet of standing water and a thriving mold colony. A neighbor told me they had never actually seen anyone at the property doing any work. We had been writing checks to the contractor in Indianapolis and getting back updates that did not match what was actually on the property. The contractor had been billing for work that nobody had performed. That is the reason you pay attention to your portfolio.

Insurance, Tax, and Permit Monitoring

Chapter 10 Part 1 covered the insurance protocol at origination and Chapter 13 covered the servicer's role in enforcing it through the life of the loan. Monitoring picks up the credit oversight piece. The lender wants to see the renewal certificates each year. The lender wants to know which policies did not renew at the same coverage. The lender wants to see force-placed coverage triggered the day the borrower's policy lapses and the borrower notified at the same moment. If those things are not happening on schedule, the lender wants to know about it from the lender's own routine rather than from a phone call after a fire.

Property taxes deserve a section of their own. Tax delinquency is the quietest risk in the portfolio because the consequences feel further out than the consequences of a missed mortgage payment. A borrower who is current with you on the loan can still be more than a year behind on the property taxes, and the tax lien sits in front of your mortgage. That is a problem you discover at the worst possible moment if you are not monitoring at the parcel level. The reasons taxes go unpaid even when the borrower is current with you vary. Cash is tight and the tax bill is large and not due monthly. The escrow account was never set up. A special assessment posted that the borrower was not expecting. The bill was sent to an old address. The borrower simply forgot. The reason does not matter as much as the discovery. The lender who pulls the parcel-level tax record once or twice a year on every property in the portfolio finds the problem when it is still a problem that can be fixed. Do you remember when we discussed recording your mortgage assignments instead of letting them sit in the file? If a property isn't being monitored closely, how else do you get notified when property taxes have not been paid?

On construction collateral, permit and inspection status belong in the monitoring routine alongside insurance and taxes. When a permit has expired, the project is no longer authorized to proceed. Trust me, you don't want to have a borrower red-tagged for unpermitted work. When an inspection has been failed and not reconciled, the project may not be able to get its certificate of occupancy. Both situations affect the lender's collateral position and the timeline to a finished, sellable asset. Neither situation will show up on the servicer's monthly report. The lender or the lender's inspector has to be checking the local permit office on a routine that fits the project.

One of our best customers learned this the expensive way. They ran a fix-and-flip operation that was growing rapidly, and their regular general contractor, who was excellent, was overbooked. They needed help carrying the volume. Enter John (the name is changed). John had done some light repair work for them in the past that had turned out fine, and he had been pressing them for more. Since their regular GC was backed up, they gave John a shot on a handful of projects the regular GC could not get to. John was not a general contractor himself. He was working under another GC. The first clue something was wrong came on one of the projects, where John installed a bathtub and forgot to install the plumbing to fill it. The fatal problem, though, was the permit. Our client always had permits pulled. Always. John swore he had pulled the permit on the project. He had not. He had lied. Work commenced. The city inspectors showed up, found work in progress without an authorized permit, and red-tagged the project. By the time the violation was sorted out, there was no path to saving what had been built. Our client had to tear the entire structure down. That single failure started a downward spiral that cost our client their flipping business. The story is not really about John. There are dishonest contractors in every market. The story is about the lender on the other side of a project like that one. The lender's permit-monitoring routine is the last line of defense against a contractor's lie that the borrower believed. If you are not checking the local permit office on your own schedule, you are only finding out about a missing permit when the city inspector shows up at the property. By that point, the project is on its way to becoming an REO, and the collateral you thought was getting built is getting torn down instead.

Behavioral Signals From the Borrower

Borrowers tell you the loan is going to default long before they actually default. The signals are not always dramatic. The borrower who used to return calls within the day starts taking three days to respond, then a week, then not at all. The tone of the emails shifts from cooperative to defensive. The payment that always arrived on the third arrives on the tenth, then the fifteenth, then not at all. The phone number on file gets disconnected. The mailing address changes. The email address changes. The borrower stops asking questions about the loan and starts asking different kinds of questions about what happens if a payment is missed. None of those signals are conclusive by themselves. Several of them stacked up over a few months are almost always the warning that something has changed.

The most reliable signal of all is the one in the Dougie Downer line at the end of this chapter. The borrower stops answering the phone before they stop paying. Keeping even a simple log of borrower communication frequency and tone catches that signal long before the default occurs. Without that log, you find out at the same time the servicer's system picks up on the missed payment.

There is another side to that coin worth telling. Early in my career, I was collecting for a lender in rural Missouri. One borrower in particular was really struggling. The loan was a large loan that had fallen severely delinquent and stayed there. What set him apart from every other delinquent borrower on my list was that he was the one who called me, not the other way around. He always returned my calls. He communicated openly about his situation. He obviously was trying. He never broke a promise. I was chastised more than once by management for carrying him as long as I did. My answer was the same every time. As long as he worked with me, I would work with him.

One day the phone rang and it was him. "I need the payoff figure on my loan." I asked, half joking, what had happened. Did he hit the lottery? That was exactly what had happened. He had won a jackpot. He told me on that call that I was the only creditor in his life who had treated him with any decency through that whole stretch, and I was the first creditor he was paying. I am a firm believer in extending grace, dignity, and kindness to all borrowers. That does not mean being a doormat. I, myself, have faced trials and tribulations, so I understand the value of grace. The borrower who lies to you, who avoids you, who breaks promises, still gets grace, but it's easier to help the borrower who is straightforward about a bad situation. Courtesy and professionalism are the practice across both kinds of conversations, and once in a while, the borrower you treated like a human being is the one who pays you first when his luck turns.

Portfolio-Level Concentration Monitoring

The risks we named in Chapter 5 do real damage in a portfolio. A working portfolio manager watches each of these categories deliberately. Borrower concentration is the first. When you have three loans to the same borrower, you are one bad event away from owning a problem portfolio. Stacking seven loans to the same borrower across two LLCs does not change the math; it just hides it behind separate entities. Market concentration is the second. If you have ten loans in one zip code, anything that hits that zip code hits your portfolio, whether it is a major employer leaving, an insurance carrier pulling out, or a hurricane. Product type concentration is the third. If your portfolio is entirely fix-and-flip, you are exposed to a slowdown in the resale market that will not show up in performance numbers until projects start finishing and not selling. Collateral category concentration is the fourth. If you are heavily weighted toward one collateral category, like small multifamily, rural single-family, hotels, or medical, the same dynamic applies.

I lived through one of these concentrations firsthand. In the early 2000s, several of my clients bought heavily into Southwest Florida. Communities like Port Charlotte and Fort Myers were booming. Waterfront lots there were more affordable than in Miami, Sarasota, or the Tampa Bay area, and the national housing boom was in full swing with Southwest Florida among the fastest growing markets in the country. In 2004, conditions in the Caribbean were particularly ripe for hurricane activity. Hurricane Charley was forecast to turn right into Tampa Bay, and many of my friends had to evacuate inland. My home became a shelter for several of them as we watched the storm inch closer to our area. At the last minute, Charley took an unexpected turn and slammed into the coast considerably south of its expected path, right into Port Charlotte. The Southwest Florida area was decimated. Losses were catastrophic. The owners and builders who were resilient chose to rebuild, but the national housing boom had already drained the country's supply of building materials. China became a major supplier of materials for the rebuild. The drywall coming out of China, however, had been manufactured with sulfuric compounds that ate the metal in copper wiring and caused respiratory issues in the people living in the rebuilt homes. That second wave of damage set Southwest Florida back years. Insurance companies, lenders, and builders took losses in the billions in that area alone. A lender whose portfolio was heavily concentrated in that one geography in 2004 did not just take a hit from the storm. They took a second hit, on the same properties, from the supply chain consequence of the storm itself. Geographic concentration is not just the headline event. It is everything that follows.

None of these concentrations are wrong in themselves. A lender who specializes in a particular market or a particular product type is going to develop concentration in that area, and that specialization is often the source of their edge. The point of the monitoring is to know the concentration is there, to price the additional risk into the rate and the structure, and to set a ceiling beyond which the concentration becomes uncomfortable. Knowing your concentration lets you manage it. If you have never measured your concentration, you are exposed without knowing it.

Building a Routine That Fits Your Operation

None of this requires a department. A private lender with a handful of loans can build a competent monitoring routine on a single spreadsheet and a calendar. The spreadsheet lists every loan with the key data: borrower, collateral, original loan amount, current balance, payment status, insurance renewal date, property tax due date, last property visit, and any notes from the most recent borrower communication. The calendar drives the routine: monthly review of the servicer's report, quarterly portfolio concentration review, scheduled property visits at intervals that fit the file size and the risk profile, annual parcel-level tax check, annual insurance certificate review. A larger operation will add a dedicated portfolio manager, a more formal monthly review, and a written portfolio policy that sets the ceilings and the triggers. The mechanics scale with the size. The principle does not change. Pick the routine that fits your operation. Run it consistently. A simple routine run consistently catches more than a sophisticated routine run once.

Dougie Downer

The borrower stops answering the phone before they stop paying. By the time the payment is late, it is often too late to do anything about it. The monitoring routine is how you find it first.

Chapter 15

Default: What To Do When Things Change

Fresh out of college, my first job at the bank was making collection calls to borrowers who were fifteen days past due. That assignment taught me as much about lending as anything I have ever done. Most new lenders come out of school and step straight into origination. My first boss had a different rule. He believed a new lender should not have loan authority until they had spent meaningful time on the collection side and understood, in their own gut, why loans go bad. It was like Mr. Miyagi telling me wax on, wax off. I did not understand what he was teaching me at the time. I figured it out quickly. The borrower fifteen days late is the best source of information a lender has about why loans go bad and what a lender can do about them while there is still time to act.

Default is a process that is a lot like watching paint dry. It is slow, it is uneven, and people who are watching it carefully see it happen long before the rest. What the lender or note holder does right after a payment is missed determines whether the loan becomes a manageable workout or a protracted and expensive fight. Most of the avoidable damage in a defaulted loan happens in the first thirty days, and almost all of it traces back to actions the lender took without thinking through the consequences.

The Sequence: Demand, Cure, and Acceleration

Almost every loan default follows the same basic legal sequence. A payment is missed. The lender sends a notice of default that identifies the missed payment, the amount required to cure, and the cure period. The borrower either cures within that period or does not. If the borrower does not cure, the lender accelerates the loan, declaring the entire unpaid balance immediately due and payable, and proceeds toward enforcement against the collateral. That is the framework. The fights happen inside the details.

The errors private lenders and note buyers most often make inside that sequence are pretty standard. They send the demand letter to the wrong address. They state the cure amount incorrectly because they did not include default interest or late charges that the note actually allowed. They send the notice from the wrong party, often the loan officer rather than the lender or the loan servicer. They miss the notice requirements in the security instrument or in state law (some states require a specific form, specific timing, or specific recipients on a default notice). They accelerate before the cure period has actually expired. They accept a partial payment after acceleration without realizing they may have just reinstated the loan. Any one of those errors hands the borrower a defense that delays enforcement and increases the cost of the workout. Read your documents. Read your state's default and acceleration statutes. Follow them precisely.

Reading the Borrower's Situation Early

A borrower who is habitually paying late is telling you something is wrong before they tell you in plain language. My practice on a borrower who has slipped into a late pattern is to ask the borrower to update their information with us. The polite framing is that we want to keep our records current. The real purpose is to look at the borrower's overall credit position with fresh eyes. When you hold a loan with a borrower, you generally have permission to pull their credit report periodically. Use that permission. Look at how the borrower is handling their other obligations and how heavy their credit card balances have become. If you see a stack of maxed-out cards, the borrower is robbing Peter to pay Paul, and you need to find a way out of the situation quickly and quietly before the other creditors figure out what is happening to them. The maxed-out cards usually precede the missed loan payment. If you are watching, you catch the problem early. If you are not, you find out about the default only after the other creditors have already started moving.

Be the First Lender to Know

I grew up in a small town in Illinois where high school basketball was a religion. In the bigger cities, you went out to restaurants, theaters, and concerts on a Friday night. In a small Illinois farm town, you had high school basketball on Tuesday and Friday nights. That was the entertainment. The town also had some amazing bakers and cooks. The two went together. At halftime of varsity games, local folks baked cakes that the school raffled for fundraisers. One of the variations was the cake walk. Numbers were placed on the floor in a circle. The crowd walked around the circle while music played, a lot like musical chairs. The music stopped, a number was drawn, and whoever was standing on that number won the cake. One year someone decided to run an actual round of musical chairs with cake as the prize. The execution did not go as well as the planners had hoped, but the principle landed for me anyway. You have to be quick. You have to grab the chair.

Collecting a loan works the same way. The lender who recognizes the problem first and addresses it first has the best chance of working out a solution that protects their position. The cash and the assets the borrower has on hand are limited. The other creditors are also watching, and the moment one of them moves, the others tend to follow. Liens get filed. Bank accounts get garnished. Judgments get entered. The lender who shows up after all of that has happened is collecting on what is left, and what is left is usually a fraction of what was there a month before.

The same principle showed up in a different form in the days when paper checks took several days to clear. Check kiting was a real and frequent problem in banks. The kiter would open several checking accounts at different banks and write checks between them in rapid succession, using the float to artificially inflate the balance in each account. It was a shell game, and it always collapsed eventually. The first bank to catch the pattern would place a hold on the account or shut it down entirely. The other banks were left holding the bag for whatever balance was outstanding when the music stopped. Check kiting is a federal crime. Missing loan payments is not, and the two situations are obviously different. What they share is that the first creditor to discover the problem is the creditor most likely to walk away whole. The creditors who discover it later are negotiating over what the first one did not already collect. That is one of the reasons early detection matters as much as it does.

The Pre-Default Conversation: Temporary or Permanent

When you reach a borrower in the days right after a missed payment, the single most important question to answer is whether the borrower's problem is temporary or permanent. A temporary problem is a job change, a medical event, a one-time business interruption, a divorce that is resolving, or a payment timing mismatch the borrower can fix within days. A permanent problem is a borrower whose underlying income or business cannot support the loan as written and will not be able to next month either. The two situations call for very different responses, and the lender who confuses them does damage in both directions. Treating a permanent problem as if it were temporary lets the borrower dig deeper into trouble while you pretend the loan is still performing. The opposite mistake, treating a temporary problem as if it were permanent, breaks a perfectly recoverable relationship and walks you into an expensive workout that was not necessary.

On a temporary problem, a small structural adjustment will sometimes resolve the situation cleanly. In my collection days I cannot tell you the number of times I would say to a borrower, "I tell you what. Come by the office. We will renew your loan, roll in three or four of your credit card balances, lower your overall monthly payment, and structure it so you will not have a payment due for thirty days. Will that help?" For a borrower with a temporary issue and a real ability to recover, that conversation saved the relationship, and often saved the borrower from a much worse outcome. You only make that offer when you have carefully assessed that the issue is temporary and the restructured terms are something the borrower can actually carry. Anything more serious is the subject of the next chapter, where workout and loss mitigation will be fully addressed.

One word of caution on any restructure or payment arrangement made at this stage. Anything you agree to with the borrower in those early conversations becomes part of the file. If the borrower later fails on the restructured terms and you find yourself in a contested workout or foreclosure, the borrower's attorney is going to argue that the original default was cured, the original notice was waived, or the new arrangement modified the original terms. Think carefully about how any payment arrangement affects the future collection process before you commit to it. Put nothing in writing that you have not thought through. Put nothing in motion that your documents and your state law do not support.

Written Communication and Recordkeeping

Every notice, every letter, every email, and every written communication with the borrower from the first late notice forward needs to be carefully drafted and carefully preserved. The default notice itself needs to come from the right party, in the right form, to the right address, with the right cure amount, on the right timeline. The records need to show that the notice was sent, when it was sent, how it was sent, and to whom. Certified mail with return receipt, or a comparable form of trackable delivery, is the standard on the formal notices that the loan documents or state law require. Email is fine for routine communication but is not a substitute for the formal notices that have to be in the file.

The other side of the recordkeeping is the conversation log. Every phone call with the borrower at this stage should be noted in the file the same day, with the date, the time, who was on the call, what was said, and any commitments made on either side. If you offer the borrower a restructure conversation, the offer goes in the file. If the borrower agrees to make a payment by a certain date, the commitment goes in the file. If the borrower asks for more time or floats a hardship explanation, those go in the file too. Be sure any offers have a deadline so you do not have open-ended offers that a client might bring up down the road when that offer no longer works. Down the road, in a workout discussion or in a deposition, the file is the record. Your memory is not. The lender who took the notes when the events were fresh has the better case.

Counsel: Getting an Opinion Versus Turning Over the File

There is a difference between calling counsel for an opinion and turning the file over to counsel for handling. Both are appropriate at different points in the default process. Getting an opinion is what you do when you have a specific question and you want a competent answer before you act. Is this notice form acceptable in this state? Does this cure amount comply with the security instrument? Does the borrower's recent payment reinstate the loan? Has the cure period actually expired given the manner of service? Those are questions you ask counsel before you move. The cost of an hour of an attorney's time on a specific question is a tiny fraction of the cost of acting on a wrong assumption.

Turning the file over is what you do when the borrower has not cured, the workout conversations have not produced a result, and the matter is heading toward enforcement. From that point, counsel runs the formal process and the lender supports counsel's work rather than the other way around. The transition between getting an opinion and turning the file over is one of the judgment calls a lender has to make on every defaulted loan. The right time to make it is generally earlier than you think it is. The cost of bringing counsel in a month before they were strictly necessary is far smaller than the cost of bringing them in a month after they should have been. Remember from earlier in this book that we discussed staying on top of your attorney to ensure they are staying on top of the file. Everyone needs to move quickly to solve problems. That includes you.

What Not to Do

The list of things not to do in the early days of a default is long, but a handful come up over and over again. Do not accept a partial payment without understanding what that payment does to your default position. In many jurisdictions and under many notes, the acceptance of a partial payment after acceleration can be argued as a reinstatement of the loan. If you accept a partial payment, you want a written acknowledgment from the borrower that the payment does not cure the default, does not waive any of the lender's rights, and is applied to the indebtedness without prejudice. Do not promise the borrower anything you have not put in writing. A verbal forbearance that is not reduced to a written agreement is an argument waiting to happen. It only takes a moment to follow up a call with a "Thanks for discussing your situation with me. Per our conversation..." email. Do not have collection conversations through unmonitored personal channels. A text message or a personal email from the lender's phone is a record the lender cannot fully control and the borrower can later mischaracterize. Do not let the cure period run past the deadline without taking the next action. A cure period that the lender allows to lapse without acceleration can be argued as a waiver of the right to accelerate on that particular default. Do not threaten actions you are not actually prepared to take. The lender who threatens foreclosure on a Monday and then does nothing about it has trained the borrower to ignore the next threat. You shouldn't be making threats anyway. We will discuss that in the next chapter. Do not communicate with the borrower in language that could be construed as harassment, deception, or unfair practice under federal or state collection law. The Fair Debt Collection Practices Act applies to certain creditors and not to others, but the general principles of fair dealing apply to everyone.

Dougie Downer

When a client starts to struggle, the signs are subtle. They have exhausted their cash and their assets, and there is limited money left to pay all of their creditors. You have to identify the issues before the other creditors do if you want a favorable outcome for your portfolio. Early detection is a must. You cannot ignore minor trouble signs. You have to act, and you have to act quickly.

Chapter 16

Workout, Loss Mitigation, and the Borrower in Bankruptcy

If I had planned this book a little better, the chapter on bankruptcy would have been Chapter 7, Chapter 11, or Chapter 13. It is none of those. It is Chapter 16. The opportunity for cleverness escaped me, and there is no taking it back now. The lesson is the same one we are about to apply to bankruptcy itself. You play the cards in front of you, not the ones you wish you had drawn.

The best outcome on a troubled loan is rarely the foreclosure. Workout is its own field of expertise, and bankruptcy is the legal framework the borrower most often reaches for when the workout discussion breaks down. The private lender or note investor needs a working understanding of both, the understanding to know which path makes sense, and the discretion to bring in experienced counsel before acting on either. The rest of this chapter walks through the workout tools available before bankruptcy, the basic structure of the three bankruptcy chapters a private lender or note investor is most likely to encounter, and the few principles that govern the secured creditor's posture in all three.

Workout First, Foreclosure Last

Foreclosure is the last exit, not the first choice. As we've said before, the collateral is the tertiary repayment method, not the primary or secondary. It is expensive, it is slow, it is uncertain, and the net recovery on a foreclosed asset is almost always lower than the recovery on a loan worked out to a result both parties can agree upon. Reaching for foreclosure as the first response to default leaves real money on the table on most files. Sitting down with the borrower, identifying the real problem, and asking what can be done to solve it puts you in a better position to recover what is recoverable.

That posture is harder than it sounds, and it takes practice. Early in my career, before I had loan authority, I was making collection calls. I had a borrower on the phone whose car loan was past due, and at some point in the call I said, "If you do not pay me, I am going to have to repossess your car." I hung up the phone feeling like I had handled it. My boss had been listening. He sat me down and said, "Let us talk about that call. What might you have done differently?" I had no idea what I had done wrong. He explained, patiently, that the borrower I had just threatened was at that very moment moving the car into a garage or over to a friend's property so the repo man could not find it. His advice was simple. Never threaten. If you have to do it, just do it. It is hard to park a piece of real estate in a garage, but the principle is the same. Threatening a borrower in a collection or workout conversation does not produce information or cooperation. It produces silence. When a borrower feels threatened, they stop returning calls. When they feel heard, they tell you the real problem, and that information is the basis of every successful workout. Listen. Shut up. Let the borrower talk. We made the same point at the end of Chapter 15. It applies even more strongly in a workout, where the goal is to keep the borrower at the table long enough to find a solution.

Forbearance Agreements

A forbearance agreement is a written contract under which the lender agrees not to enforce its remedies for a defined period of time, in exchange for defined commitments from the borrower. The borrower may agree to bring the loan current over a cure schedule, deliver additional collateral, provide updated financial information, sign a confession of judgment in jurisdictions that recognize them, or perform some other action that gives the lender a better position than the lender had before the agreement was signed. The lender, in return, agrees to hold off on default-related enforcement during the forbearance period.

A properly drafted forbearance agreement identifies the existing default with specificity, acknowledges the default in writing, preserves all of the lender's rights with respect to that default and any future default, defines the borrower's cure obligations and the timeline, identifies any new collateral or guaranties being added, and states the consequences of a failure to perform under the forbearance itself. The most common drafting errors that make a forbearance agreement unenforceable or commercially useless are the failure to name the default being forborne (so the borrower argues later that the agreement covered a broader range of conduct), the failure to preserve future-default rights (so the borrower argues later that the forbearance modified the underlying note), the failure to require a written acknowledgment of the debt and the default (so the borrower argues later that the debt was disputed), and the failure to address the lender's right to revoke the forbearance if any other event of default occurs during the period. Get the document drafted by an attorney who actually does this in your jurisdiction. A forbearance agreement that does not hold up is worse than no agreement at all, because it commits the lender to a period of inaction without securing the protections the lender thought it had.

Loan Modifications

A loan modification is a permanent change to the terms of the original note. The interest rate, the payment, the maturity date, the amortization, or some combination get rewritten and the borrower commits to the new terms going forward. A modification is appropriate when the underlying credit situation has changed in a way that the original terms cannot be met but the borrower can meet the modified terms over the long term. A modification is not appropriate when the borrower's situation is short-term, when the borrower cannot meet the modified terms either, or when the modification amounts to avoiding a workout conversation that needs to happen.

Whatever you give up in a modification, get something back. A reduced interest rate gets matched with additional collateral, a personal guarantee, a shorter term, or another concession on the borrower's side. A reduced payment gets matched with the same kind of consideration. A modification that gives the borrower everything they asked for in exchange for nothing the lender did not already have tells the borrower they can come back at a later date and ask again.

A modification that increases the loan amount, extends the maturity, or substantively changes the obligation can affect your lien position with respect to junior lienholders and can affect your title insurance coverage. The general rule is that a modification recorded as a modification of the existing mortgage preserves the lien position. A modification that is in substance a refinance can be argued by junior lienholders as having changed the priority. Chapter 10 Part 1 walked through the title policy mechanics at origination. The same questions apply to a modification. Talk to your title attorney before recording. Get a date-down endorsement or a modification endorsement from the title company where the file requires it. Do not assume that the modification you negotiated with the borrower keeps you in the same lien position you held before.

Deed in Lieu of Foreclosure

A deed in lieu of foreclosure is a transaction in which the borrower voluntarily conveys the collateral to the lender in satisfaction of the loan, in whole or in part. It is faster than foreclosure, cheaper than foreclosure, and usually cleaner than foreclosure. It only works when a handful of conditions are met.

The first condition is that there are no other liens against the property whose effect on the new owner the lender has not analyzed. A deed in lieu does not cleanse the title of junior liens the way a foreclosure does. The lender taking a deed in lieu takes the property subject to every encumbrance that the deed in lieu does not address. Junior mortgages, mechanic's liens, judgment liens, tax liens, and HOA liens all survive the transfer unless they are released or otherwise resolved as part of the transaction. A clean deed in lieu on a property with junior liens is not actually clean. The second condition is that the borrower understands and agrees in writing that the conveyance is a voluntary transfer in satisfaction of the debt to the extent the parties define. The third condition is that the deficiency, if any, is handled explicitly, either through a written waiver by the lender or through an express reservation of the lender's right to pursue it. Leaving the deficiency question unaddressed is how disputes start. The fourth condition is that the borrower is advised in writing to seek independent counsel before signing, and ideally has done so. A deed in lieu signed under duress, or by a borrower who can later argue the transaction was unconscionable, is a deed in lieu the borrower's attorney is going to try to unwind. You'll also want to advise the borrower to consult their tax professional as a deed in lieu often involves a forgiveness of debt, which might be taxable income to the borrower.

Credit reporting on a deed in lieu is its own conversation. The lender can typically report the loan as paid through deed in lieu, paid in full through deed in lieu, or settled for less than the full balance depending on what the parties actually agreed to. The borrower will often ask the lender to report the loan as paid in full. The lender has to make an accurate reporting decision based on what actually happened. In note circles, there is a lot of disagreement on how to report deeds in lieu on the credit report. I implore you to speak with your attorney about how this should be handled.

Receivership, Short Payoffs, Discounted Payoffs, and Selling the Note

Several other workout tools go along with the forbearance, the modification, and the deed in lieu. Receivership is the appointment by a court of a neutral third party to manage the collateral property during a dispute or workout, collect rents, pay necessary expenses, and preserve the asset until the matter is resolved. Receivership is most useful on income property where the borrower has stopped managing the asset competently and the property is deteriorating in real time. The receiver's costs are typically paid out of the property's cash flow or added to the loan balance under the security instrument. The procedural rules vary by state, and a receivership requires court action and counsel.

A short payoff, also known as a short sale, is a workout in which the lender accepts less than the full unpaid balance in satisfaction of the loan, usually because the collateral cannot support the full balance and the borrower cannot make up the difference. A discounted payoff is the same transaction described from a slightly different angle. Both require careful documentation, careful tax consideration on the borrower side because the cancellation of indebtedness can be income to the borrower, and careful credit reporting decisions on the lender side. Both also require the lender to make a careful assessment of what a foreclosure would actually recover, because the comparison the short payoff has to beat is not the unpaid balance. It is the net recovery from the next-best alternative, after attorney fees, carrying costs, default interest that may or may not be collectible, and the time value of the money tied up in the workout.

Selling the note to a third party is a workout tool that gets used less often than it should. A lender holding a nonperforming or subperforming loan that does not want to manage the workout can sell the note to a buyer who does. The price reflects the file as it sits today, not the file as it was at origination, and the due diligence the buyer performs looks a lot like the due diligence we will cover in Chapter 19 and Chapter 20 when we get to the note market. The point for this chapter is that selling the note is a legitimate workout option, and on certain files it produces a better result for the original lender than continuing to hold a loan they are not equipped to work out. I suspect note buyers are one of the main groups of readers for this book.

When the Workout Conversation Stops Working

Even the most experienced workout specialists do not produce a result on every file. The borrower might not engage. The borrower might disappear. The financial situation might be worse than the borrower disclosed. The collateral might be in worse condition than originally documented. The borrower's other creditors might have moved and there is no longer enough cash or collateral to support a workout that resolves the lender's position. At some point on those files, the workout conversation stops working and the matter moves toward enforcement or toward bankruptcy. The transition is not always the lender's choice. Often it is the borrower's and they often file for bankruptcy protection.

Bankruptcy Basics and the Automatic Stay

A bankruptcy filing under any chapter of the federal Bankruptcy Code triggers an automatic stay. The automatic stay is exactly what it sounds like. The moment the petition is filed, almost every collection action, enforcement action, and creditor action against the debtor or the debtor's property comes to an immediate halt. The pending foreclosure stops. The pending lawsuit stops. The collection calls stop. The repossession crews stop. The eviction stops. The wage garnishment stops. The bank account levy stops. Continuing to take action against a debtor in bankruptcy without proper authority from the bankruptcy court is a violation of the automatic stay, and the consequences include sanctions and actual damages. The first thing every secured creditor does the moment they learn of a bankruptcy filing is stop. Then they call counsel.

The three chapters of the Bankruptcy Code a private lender or note investor is most likely to encounter are Chapter 7, Chapter 13, and Chapter 11. Each one operates differently, treats the secured creditor differently, and produces a different range of outcomes. The next three sections walk through each at a basic level. None of what follows is a substitute for the advice of experienced bankruptcy counsel on a specific case.

Chapter 7: Liquidation

Chapter 7 is liquidation. A consumer debtor under Chapter 7 surrenders nonexempt assets to a court-appointed trustee, the trustee converts those assets to cash, the cash is distributed to creditors under the priority scheme of the Bankruptcy Code, and the debtor receives a discharge of dischargeable debts at the end of the case. An entity debtor under Chapter 7 ceases operations, surrenders all assets to a trustee, and is liquidated rather than reorganized. A consumer Chapter 7 typically runs four to six months from filing to discharge. An entity Chapter 7 can run longer depending on the complexity of the asset disposition.

The secured creditor's position in a Chapter 7 is straightforward but worth understanding. The automatic stay applies. The trustee makes a determination on each piece of secured collateral. The trustee may sell the collateral free and clear of liens under the appropriate Bankruptcy Code section, in which case the lien attaches to the proceeds at the appropriate priority and the secured creditor is paid from that pool. The trustee may abandon the collateral back to the debtor as having no equity for the estate, in which case the secured creditor can pursue enforcement after the case is closed or after obtaining relief from stay. The trustee may also hand the collateral over to the secured creditor directly through the abandonment process. The secured creditor works with the trustee through counsel. The unsecured deficiency, if any, is discharged at the end of the case as to the consumer debtor. The lien on the collateral itself generally survives the bankruptcy, which is one of the principles a secured creditor needs to be operationally clear about. The personal liability of the consumer debtor is discharged. The lien is not.

Chapter 13: Individual Reorganization with Regular Income

Chapter 13 is the reorganization chapter for individuals with regular income. The debtor proposes a repayment plan, usually three to five years long, under which the debtor's disposable income is paid to a Chapter 13 trustee and distributed to creditors according to the plan. The plan has to be confirmed by the bankruptcy court, and once confirmed it binds both the debtor and the creditors with respect to the treatment of their claims. The debtor receives a discharge at the completion of the plan.

When I was a lender in St. Louis, there was an attorney in that market who advertised on television that he filed more Chapter 13 "wage earner plans" than any other attorney in the area. My understanding is that he may still hold the regional record. His advertising never used the word bankruptcy. It used the phrase "wage earner plan." Many of his clients were people doing their best to handle a difficult situation honorably, and they would call me after filing because they did not understand that filing a wage earner plan was filing bankruptcy. I would explain that I could no longer talk with them about the loan because of the automatic stay, and they would push back. "I did not file bankruptcy. I filed a wage earner plan." Although that law office seemed to gloss over the fact that it was a bankruptcy, the reality was that the moment the petition is filed, the automatic stay applies.

For a secured creditor on residential mortgage collateral, a Chapter 13 filing is often not the disaster it sounds like at first. The court takes a portion of the debtor's wages and pays creditors out of that pool. As a secured creditor on the home the debtor wants to keep, you generally get paid through the plan. The plan typically requires the debtor to cure the pre-petition arrearage through the plan over the three to five year period while staying current on the post-petition payments outside the plan. Late charges, default interest, and certain other amounts can be included in the arrearage cure depending on how the plan is drafted and what your loan documents and applicable law allow. For a note investor holding a nonperforming real estate-backed loan, a Chapter 13 can be a path to monthly payment, gradual cure of the arrearage, and a performing loan down the road. That is not always how it works, and a plan that the debtor cannot complete results in dismissal or conversion to Chapter 7. Those conversions are common. On the right file, though, a Chapter 13 is one of the better outcomes available to a secured creditor on a defaulted loan.

Chapter 11: Business Reorganization

Chapter 11 is the business reorganization chapter. Operating companies, partnerships, LLCs, and individuals with substantial business interests use Chapter 11 to reorganize under court supervision. The debtor typically operates as the debtor in possession, runs the business through the case, proposes a plan of reorganization that addresses the treatment of all creditors, and asks the court to confirm that plan. A streamlined small business Chapter 11 can move in months. A contested complex Chapter 11 can run for years.

The secured creditor's posture in a Chapter 11 is more complicated than in Chapter 7 or Chapter 13 and is genuinely something that belongs to an attorney rather than to the lender trying to DIY it. The secured creditor preserves the collateral, monitors the case, files a proof of claim, evaluates the plan when it is proposed, and votes the claim. The secured creditor can sometimes seek relief from the automatic stay if the collateral is not adequately protected, if there is no equity in the property and the property is not necessary to an effective reorganization, or if other specified grounds apply. The motion for relief from stay is the single most important early action a secured creditor sometimes takes in a Chapter 11. It is also not the kind of motion you draft from a template you found online. Get counsel who actually practices bankruptcy from a creditor's perspective in the district where the case is filed.

Notice of Filing and the Proof of Claim

In every bankruptcy chapter, the secured creditor receives a notice of the filing and is given a deadline to file a proof of claim. The proof of claim is a written statement asserting the amount and nature of the claim and the basis for the claim. The deadline to file is set by the court at the beginning of the case and is enforced strictly. A claim filed late is a claim that may not be paid. The proof of claim has to be supported by the underlying loan documents, including the note, the security instrument, the recorded assignments where applicable, and the accounting that supports the balance asserted. A defective proof of claim can be objected to by the trustee, by the debtor, or by other creditors, and the resolution of those objections is part of why the secured creditor coordinates with counsel through the case rather than filing the claim from a template and waiting to see what happens.

Hire Experienced Counsel at the Moment of Filing

The single most important decision a private lender or note investor makes in a bankruptcy case is to retain experienced creditor-rights bankruptcy counsel at the moment of filing rather than read the Bankruptcy Code and respond on your own. Bankruptcy is its own body of law, with its own procedural rules, its own local rules in each district, its own customs and practices in each chamber, and its own time-tested traps for the unwary creditor. An attorney who actually represents secured creditors in real cases will know things about the local trustee, the local judges, and the local bar that no amount of reading is going to teach. The cost of competent counsel on a bankruptcy file is a fraction of the cost of missing a deadline, mis-filing a claim, or violating the automatic stay because the lender thought they could handle the matter on their own. Make the call the day you get the notice.

Dougie Downer

The borrower's bankruptcy filing is not the end of the lender's position. It is the time the lender needs counsel who has done this exact kind of case before. The lender who tries to read the code and answer on their own is buying themselves an outcome they will not enjoy.

Chapter 17

Foreclosure and REO: Getting the Collateral Back

We took over a very low-end portfolio in the Mid-Atlantic some years ago, and one of the assets was a run-down duplex with serious code violation issues. Before we filed any paperwork to foreclose, we did the analysis on the exit. The back taxes owed were significant. The code violation fines had been stacking up for years. The renovation cost to bring the property to a condition we could actually sell was substantial. When we added the three numbers to the cost of the foreclosure and the cost of carrying and disposing of the asset, the all-in figure was materially higher than the ARV in any realistic scenario. Taking the property back would have produced a loss on a loan that was already a loss. We charged the loan off instead. It was the right economic decision.

Before you commit to foreclosing on a piece of collateral, the first question is whether you should foreclose at all. Understanding what you are about to take back is part of the analysis, not an afterthought. The rest of this chapter walks through what foreclosure actually looks like in practice, what the lender does with the property after taking it back, and a hint of what the process of running an REO portfolio is actually like. Owning the asset after foreclosure is a separate part of the job, and the skill set required to do it well has very little overlap with the skill set required to lend.

Foreclosure is the last exit on a troubled loan. It is slow, it is expensive, it is distasteful to take a property away from someone who owns it, and the net recovery rarely looks like the gross balance the lender carries on the books. Chapter 16 walked through the workout tools available before the foreclosure complaint is filed. This chapter assumes those tools have either been used or are not available.

A Word on Lien Theory vs Deed Theory

Chapter 8 walked through the two models for securing real estate debt in the United States, lien theory and deed theory. The distinction determines how the lender takes the collateral back. A lien theory state runs the lender through a judicial foreclosure. A deed theory state runs the lender through a non-judicial foreclosure conducted by the trustee under the deed of trust. The substance of the protection is similar. The procedure is very different. Rather than re-walk the framework here, I will assume Chapter 8 is still fresh on your mind and concentrate on what each process actually feels like in practice.

What a Judicial Foreclosure Actually Looks Like

A judicial foreclosure is a lawsuit, and it moves at the speed of the court that hears it. The lender hires foreclosure counsel licensed in the state where the collateral sits, counsel files a complaint, and the case proceeds through the same litigation calendar as everything else in front of that judge. The borrower is served. The borrower files an answer. The case grinds through discovery, motions, a hearing or trial, a judgment of foreclosure, a sheriff's sale, a redemption period in many jurisdictions, court confirmation, and finally delivery of a deed to the successful bidder. None of it is fast.

Timelines range from a few months on the friendly end to several years on the contested end. Where you land depends on the borrower, on the borrower's counsel, and on the condition of your loan file. A clean file with sound documentation moves through the calendar without inviting argument. A weak file invites every defense in the book, and there are plenty of them. Standing to enforce the note. Gaps in the assignment chain. A notarization the borrower questions. The proof of default. Various consumer protection arguments under state and federal law. None of those defenses are unusual. None are fatal to a clean file. All of them can extend the case by months when the file has holes. That is one of the practical reasons the documentation chapter applies directly here.

Borrowers with patient counsel also know how to stretch a case in other ways. They request a continuance to pursue a modification. They file for bankruptcy on the eve of a hearing. They change counsel and the new attorney needs time to come up to speed. A borrower passes away mid-case and the estate has to be opened. A spouse surfaces claiming a homestead interest the original action did not address. Each event stops the clock. A patient borrower with competent counsel can keep a judicial foreclosure tied up well past anything that resembles a reasonable resolution.

Through all of that, hire competent foreclosure counsel and let them do the job. A lender who tries to direct litigation strategy from a position of inexperience makes the case longer, makes it more expensive, and creates appellate problems no one sees coming. That said, the lender's job does not end at hiring the attorney. Stay on top of the file. Confirm the calendar is moving. There are great foreclosure attorneys in this work and there are weaker ones, and the difference shows up in months on the back end.

What a Non-Judicial Foreclosure Actually Looks Like

A non-judicial foreclosure is not a lawsuit, and that single fact changes almost everything about how the process feels in practice. The deed of trust contains a power of sale provision that authorizes the trustee, on default and the lender's instruction, to conduct a sale under the procedures defined by state statute. Those procedures vary state by state but typically require notice of default, notice of intent to sell, publication of the notice of sale for a prescribed period, and the sale itself at a defined location on a defined schedule. The trustee, not a judge, conducts the sale. The successful bidder receives a trustee's deed.

The whole thing closes faster and costs less. Some deed of trust states can finish the process in a matter of months when there is no contest and no bankruptcy filing. Counsel is still essential, and in most of the cases we have worked in deed theory states our attorney steps in as the substitute trustee so they drive the sale themselves. Most lenders work this way.

The most common complication is exactly what you would expect. The borrower files for bankruptcy on the eve of the sale. The automatic stay we covered in Chapter 16 freezes everything. A foreclosure sale set for a Tuesday morning regularly gets stayed by a petition filed late Monday afternoon. Borrowers and their attorneys know this, and the lender's counsel needs to be ready to move the moment the filing lands.

Bankruptcy in the Foreclosure Process

Chapter 16 covered the secured creditor's position in each of the three bankruptcy chapters most likely to be encountered by a private lender. The two procedural mechanics most relevant to foreclosure are the automatic stay and the motion for relief from stay. The automatic stay halts foreclosure activity the moment the petition is filed. The motion for relief from stay is the secured creditor's tool for obtaining permission from the bankruptcy court to proceed notwithstanding the stay. The motion is granted where the debtor has no equity in the property and the property is not necessary for an effective reorganization, or where the debtor has failed to provide adequate protection of the lender's secured interest. This belongs to experienced bankruptcy counsel. The lender who tries to navigate a motion for relief from stay without counsel is buying themselves a result they will not enjoy.

Recovering Attorney Fees, Default Interest, and Carrying Costs

Most private loan documents drafted by a competent attorney include language that allows the lender to recover the cost of enforcement, including reasonable attorney fees, default interest, advances for taxes and insurance, advances for property preservation, and other carrying costs incurred during the default and foreclosure period. Whether the lender actually recovers those amounts depends on two things. First, the documents have to provide for the recovery in language that is enforceable in the jurisdiction. Second, the equity in the property has to be sufficient to support the recovery after the principal balance is paid.

In an equity case where the property is worth materially more than the principal balance, the lender stands a reasonable chance of recovering most of the default interest, the attorney fees, and the advances. In a deficiency case where the property is worth less than the principal balance, those additional amounts go onto the deficiency claim against the borrower, which may or may not be collectible depending on the borrower's financial position and the jurisdiction's deficiency law. A lender planning to recover full enforcement costs on every foreclosed loan will be disappointed in a meaningful number of cases. Without documents that provide for the recovery in the first place, the disappointment is universal.

The Deed in Lieu as an Alternative to Foreclosure

We touched on the deed in lieu in Chapter 16 as a workout tool. It belongs in this chapter as well, because in the world of foreclosure and REO, the deed in lieu is often the best available alternative to a contested judicial foreclosure that drags on for years.

The structure I want to highlight here is the deed in lieu with a deficiency waiver in exchange for the borrower delivering the property in broom-swept condition. The borrower is embarrassed. The borrower cannot pay. The borrower wants out. The lender wants the property back without spending well over a year in litigation. A negotiated transaction in which the borrower signs the deed, hands over the keys, leaves the property clean and undamaged, and walks away with a written waiver of the deficiency satisfies both sides. The lender saves the time value of money on the foreclosure timeline, saves the attorney fees, saves the carrying costs through the litigation period, and takes a property that has not been stripped or damaged on the way out. The borrower saves their credit from further damage, walks away with closure on the obligation, and avoids the dignity cost of being sued.

When we started Castle Rock back in 2007 and 2008, in part to buy severely delinquent nonperforming residential and commercial mortgage loans coming out of the bank market, we worked through an enormous number of those conversations. I cannot recall a single instance from those years in which a borrower who was in regular contact with us and who was willing to engage actually went all the way through a contested foreclosure. The vast majority of troubled borrowers want to find a solution. The most common solution they offer is the deed in lieu. The lender's job is to be professional, to extend empathy and grace to an embarrassed customer, and to give the borrower a way out that is not punitive. The borrowers who cooperate get deeds in lieu and walk away. The borrowers we ended up foreclosing on were the borrowers who disappeared, the borrowers whose counsel directed them to fight, and the rare friendly foreclosure done by mutual agreement to clear a title that a deed in lieu could not reach.

Foreclosure does more than transfer title to the lender. It cleans the title of most of the junior liens recorded after the foreclosing mortgage. Sometimes you have to go through the process not because the borrower is fighting you but because it is the only way to clear the encumbrances behind your loan. That reality is why a friendly foreclosure is a real tool. The borrower wants the obligation done. The lender wants clear title. The structure of the foreclosure delivers both, where a deed in lieu cannot.

The Handoff from Foreclosure Counsel to Asset Management

When the foreclosure is complete and the lender owns the property, the file moves out of foreclosure counsel's hands and into the lender's asset management function. The handoff is not just a folder change. The records to include in the REO file are the deed conveying title to the lender, the title insurance policy with the endorsements appropriate to the new ownership, the foreclosure file itself with the underlying judgment or trustee's deed, the final accounting of the foreclosure costs the lender has paid and is entitled to recover from the proceeds of any future sale, any keys or codes recovered from the property, any inspection reports run during the foreclosure period, and the full underwriting file from origination forward. The REO manager who takes the asset without a complete file inherits the same kind of problem the note investor inherits when they buy a portfolio with documentation holes. Build the handoff package. Confirm it is complete before the file leaves foreclosure counsel.

Asset Management In House Versus Outsourced

Most private lenders contract out asset management. They use a third-party REO firm to secure the property, list it, manage the sale process, and handle the disposition. The arrangement works for lenders whose volume does not justify an in-house team and whose internal expertise sits in origination and servicing rather than in asset management. The trade-off is that the contracted manager is making decisions and incurring costs on behalf of the lender, and the lender's leverage over the quality of those decisions and the level of those costs is limited.

We handle asset management in house. We have for a long time. We have become really, really good at it. Asset management is unglamorous. The margin between doing it well and doing it poorly is the difference between a profitable portfolio and an unprofitable one, and the experience that comes from working through years of these cases does not transfer easily to a third-party firm whose primary loyalty is to its own billing. A lender contemplating whether to build the function in house should look carefully at portfolio volume, staffing, geographic footprint, and appetite for the function. A lender who outsources should pick a manager with a track record, set clear expectations on cost and timing, and monitor closely.

Watching the Asset Managers

A contracted asset manager bills for time and expense. The structure of the engagement, by its nature, creates an incentive to bill more time and to push more expense through the file. Some firms are disciplined about that. Many are not. The lender who takes the manager's invoice at face value, month after month, without reviewing the work product against the billing, ends up with carrying costs that materially exceed what the asset actually required.

The practice I would suggest is the same one a credit officer applies to any third-party invoice in a workout file. Read the entries. Compare the entries to the work product. Ask the manager what was done, by whom, and why. A property that has been listed for a long time, that has not had a price reduction, that has not had a marketing refresh, and that is generating a steady stream of preservation invoices is a property where someone is being paid to maintain the status quo rather than to move the asset. The lender's job is to insist that the manager either move the asset or explain, in writing, why they are not.

Securing the Asset

As soon as you gain REO ownership, you secure the property. The local agent or contractor representing the lender meets the locksmith on site, changes the locks, walks the interior, and reports the actual condition. The lender's representative on site is the most important person on the file at that time. Their report determines what the lender knows about the asset, the cost the lender is going to incur to preserve and prepare it, and the risk the lender carries between possession and disposition.

We had a foreclosure complete in a midwestern city where the agent we used met our locksmith at the property to change the locks. The home was a two-story residence with no furniture visible on the first floor. As they worked on the lock, a gentleman came to the door and claimed he was renting the home. The first floor was empty, but he had been living in the back of the second floor, out of sight, while the foreclosure ran. He was a squatter. Squatters are a recurring problem in REO work, and in most jurisdictions they are much harder to remove than they should be. The agent put him on the phone with me. I listened to his story about a lease and being a victim, and I told him politely that we would be back at the same time the following day with the local authorities, and that he might want to consider being gone before then. He was gone the next day. The outcome was favorable in that case, and it is the exception. Most squatter situations require a separate legal process to remove the occupant, and most jurisdictions provide the occupant with meaningful procedural protections. Do not count on that outcome. The story is a reminder that you do not get the chance to control the asset if you do not show up to take possession quickly.

That case taught me something else about vacant properties. We stopped putting real estate signs in front of vacant homes. We stopped leaving visible lockboxes on the door. Both of those advertise to the neighborhood that no one is living in the house. We now place portable security cameras inside vacant properties so we can see whether anyone has moved in between visits. We also use lamps on timers to make the property appear occupied. The cost is small. The information is valuable. The reason we do it is not paranoia. The reason we do it is that we have, in real cases over the years, found people living in our properties who do not belong there.

In a different midwestern town we worked through a foreclosure on an abandoned property. We did not own the property yet, so we did not have the right to enter the structure. Our agent walked the perimeter to confirm the property was secure. Shortly after that walk, we received a citation from the city for code violations inside the home. The inspector's note said that the door was open, so he just walked in. Our agent went back to the property. The local code enforcement officer had broken the glass on the back door to gain entry, and that was how the door had become open. The point of that story, beyond my opinion of that town's code enforcement office, is that the lender's position before title transfers is operationally constrained. The lender's options for protecting an abandoned property during the foreclosure period are limited, and the lender is exposed to costs imposed by local authorities that the lender did not cause.

Around the same time in the same town, we completed a foreclosure on a separate property and met our locksmith at the home. Our agent called from the property to tell me there was a classic Corvette in mint condition under a cover in the garage, with a padlock on the door. The rest of the home was abandoned. The agent gave me the VIN. I called the local police. The car was stolen, and the person I spoke with said someone would come out in a few days. I told them that once we changed the locks, the car would be gone overnight. They did not come. The car was gone in the morning, along with our broken padlock. The point of that story is not the car. The point of that story is that the asset you take possession of is rarely just the structure. People hide things in vacant homes.

The BPO Problem

Early in our company's history, our default process for getting a current value on an REO asset was the Broker's Price Opinion, the BPO. We stopped using BPOs the way we used to. The quality of those reports, across the firms and the agents who provide them, is far below what a lender needs to make decisions on real money.

We had a property come back to us through a foreclosure, and the BPO in our file described a cute, well-maintained home in a settled neighborhood. We sent one of our local contractor partners out to walk the property before we acted on the BPO. The reality was a roof partially covered with a blue tarp and a hole someone had cut through the side wall with a chainsaw, opened from the outside to pull copper out of the framing. The BPO agent had not been to the property. The photos in the report had been pulled from older online listings of the same address. The cute home in the report was the home as it had appeared at some earlier point. The home our contractor walked was a structure that needed an emergency tarp replacement, a wall repair, a full electrical inspection, and a complete renovation before anyone could safely market it.

What we use instead is a property condition report from someone with construction experience. A general contractor or an experienced rehabber walks the property, evaluates the structure, the systems, the roof, the foundation, the interior finish condition, and the immediate health and safety issues, and gives the lender a report that reflects what they actually saw. The cost is in the same range as a BPO. The information is far more useful for the decision the lender has to make. A BPO answers the question of what the price is. A construction-based condition report answers the question of what the actual condition of the asset is.

There are BPO firms and individual agents who do this the right way. They visit the property. They take their own photos. They check the comparable sales. They produce a report a lender can rely on. Those firms and those agents exist. The problem is that the lender cannot tell, from inside the BPO format, whether the report was produced from a real site visit or generated from a desk. The construction-based condition report puts the inspection in the hands of someone whose value is in what they can see when they walk through a structure.

Boots on the Ground

A theme runs through every story I have just told. The lender's outcome on a foreclosure and on the REO that follows is determined, in the field, by the person physically at the property representing the lender. That person is the agent, the contractor, the inspector, the locksmith, and the neighbor who walks by every day. The lender chooses who that person is, and the lender deals with the consequences of that choice.

The boots on the ground have to be trusted. They have to show up. They have to communicate openly about what they see. They have to be willing to push back on the lender when the lender's plan does not match the conditions in the field. They have to be available on short notice when something happens at the property. The relationship can't be transactional. The relationship is built over time, by working through real situations together, and by holding the person accountable for the quality of their work.

You also have to watch the boots. Trusted does not mean unsupervised. A contractor who is supposed to be checking on a property weekly may not be checking weekly. An agent who is supposed to be marketing the asset may not be marketing it. The lender's job is to inspect what they expect, on a schedule that is realistic but firm enough to surface a problem before the problem turns expensive.

Listing, Disposition, and the Real Carrying Cost

The disposition of an REO asset is the sale of the property to a third party. The listing price is set based on the actual condition report and the local market, not on what was owed on the foreclosed note. The buyer is usually a local investor, an owner-occupant looking for a value purchase, or a fund that buys properties in bulk. The lender's expectation should be that disposition takes longer than the lender wants and that the all-in cost of carrying the asset to disposition is meaningfully higher than the lender forecasts at the start.

The real carrying cost of an REO asset includes property tax payments brought current, hazard insurance maintained on the structure, utilities kept on long enough to support inspections and showings, lawn and landscape maintenance, snow removal where applicable, occasional repair items that surface during the holding period, the asset manager's monthly fee where applicable, listing agent commissions at the sale, closing costs at the sale, and any concessions made to the buyer to close the transaction. Those items often aren't cheap, and all of them must be accounted for when you budget for the disposition. Lenders who model the holding cost of an REO as a small percentage of the property value, paid for a short period, consistently understate the actual number. A realistic model assumes a longer hold than expected and a heavier expense run than expected, and the lender prices into the original loan, through its rate, points, and structure, the expectation that some percentage of the portfolio is going to go this way.

Back to the Question We Started With

Not every foreclosure is worth completing. The duplex at the start of this chapter was an example of that on one particular file. The same math applies on every troubled loan that we've had to work out. Add the cost to take the property back, the cost to carry it, and the cost to dispose of it. Compare the total to what the property is going to bring at sale. If recovery costs more than recovery yields, the responsible answer is to recognize the loss, take it cleanly, and put the file behind you. Stubbornness is expensive.

Dougie Downer

Just as an army would not invade a position without first running reconnaissance, the lender should not commit to a foreclosure path without first researching the exit. Choose the strategy on the bad loan based on what the field will actually allow. Pick the boots on the ground you trust, and then watch them. Losses in a workout situation are not avoided by good intentions. Losses are avoided by knowing the asset, knowing the jurisdiction, and knowing the people working on your behalf.

Part Five

Special Situations

Part Five covers the corners of this business that are not standard lending to a standard borrower. The self-directed IRA has its own set of rules and one wrong move disqualifies the account. Buying notes is a different decision than originating loans, whether the notes are performing or nonperforming. Running a private lending fund is running a small bank without a charter. And the licensing, usury, and securities rules behind all of it are easy to miss until a regulator points one of them out.

The chapters that follow take each one in turn. By the end of Part Five the reader should know enough about each to operate in these areas correctly or know enough to stay out.

Chapter 18

Lending From a Self-Directed IRA Without Disqualifying the Account

Lending from a self-directed IRA is legal, it is useful, and it is completely unforgiving of errors. The mistakes in this corner of private credit are almost always the same mistakes. The consequences almost always include disqualification of the account and a tax bill that hits all at once. This chapter walks through what a private lender holding loans inside a self-directed IRA needs to know to avoid the failures that recur in this market. It also walks through the opportunity on the other side of the table, the opportunity to lend to another person's self-directed IRA, which most institutional lenders will not touch and which a disciplined private lender can underwrite well.

Disqualified Persons and the Prohibited Transaction Rules

The Internal Revenue Code defines a set of people, called disqualified persons, with whom the IRA cannot transact. The IRA owner is a disqualified person to the IRA itself. So is the IRA owner's spouse, the owner's lineal ascendants and descendants, the spouses of those lineal ascendants and descendants, and certain fiduciaries and service providers to the IRA. Entities controlled by any of those people are also disqualified persons to the IRA, with control measured by a fifty percent ownership or beneficial interest test. Brothers, sisters, aunts, uncles, nieces, nephews, and cousins are not disqualified persons under the statute, which surprises people who assume the rule covers all family.

The edge cases most commonly misunderstood are at the controlled-entity line. An LLC the IRA owner controls is a disqualified person. One key is to think of you and your IRA as two separate living, breathing entities. There is a clear line of demarcation where one ends and the other begins. They are truly separate. An LLC the IRA owner does not control but in which they hold a significant minority interest may or may not be a disqualified person depending on the facts. An LLC the IRA owner's father controls is a disqualified person. An LLC the IRA owner's brother controls is not. A loan from the IRA to a disqualified person is a prohibited transaction. A loan from the IRA to a non-disqualified person who happens to be the IRA owner's sibling is not. The lines are precise. They do not move based on intent.

Self-Benefit, Personal Use, and the Subtler Traps

A prohibited transaction is broader than a loan to a disqualified person. The statute also prohibits the IRA from selling, exchanging, or leasing property to a disqualified person, from extending credit to a disqualified person, from furnishing goods or services to a disqualified person, from transferring or using IRA assets for the benefit of a disqualified person, and from any act by a fiduciary by which the fiduciary deals with the assets in their own interest. The phrase to learn here is the second to last one. Self-benefit by the IRA owner, even where no direct disqualified-person transaction is involved, is itself a prohibited transaction. The IRS reads that language broadly.

In private lending, the personal-use trap is most likely to surface in three places. The first is the IRA owner making a loan to a borrower where the loan terms include some non-monetary benefit to the IRA owner, such as a side promise of property use, a discounted personal transaction, or any other consideration that flows back to the natural person outside the IRA. The second is the IRA owner servicing the IRA's loans personally and paying themselves for that work. The third is the IRA owner using their own property as a place to store or process IRA records or operations. None of those activities looks dramatic. All of them can trigger a prohibited transaction finding under audit.

The Custodian Relationship

Every self-directed IRA must be held by a qualified custodian. The custodian holds the assets, processes contributions and distributions, files the required reports with the IRS, and provides the IRA with its legal status as a retirement account. The custodian does not, in most cases, evaluate the soundness of the investments held inside the IRA. The custodian's job is to process the transactions the IRA owner directs and to confirm that those transactions are administratively complete. The custodian is not the IRA owner's investment advisor. The custodian is not the IRA owner's prohibited transaction lawyer. The custodian is the recordkeeper.

We do a fair amount of work with investors who are moving old 401(k) balances into real estate and private credit. The first step is rolling those funds to a self-directed IRA custodian. There are several custodians in the market, and I know several of them. All have strengths and weaknesses. The three things I look for in a custodian are fee structure, consistency, and responsiveness.

The first is fee structure. Most custodians charge a base account fee and then charge separately for transactions, the so-called gate fees that move money in and out of the account. The fee structures vary, but most fall into a similar range. Compare them, understand them, and pick the structure that fits the volume and complexity of the activity the IRA is going to run.

The second, and to me the more important, is consistency. How often does the custodian change its fee schedule, its policies, and its procedures. If the IRA is investing in something long term, such as private loans, notes, or real estate, the IRA owner cannot have the rules changing under them every few months. A custodian that runs a stable program is worth more than a custodian with a slightly lower fee and a habit of repricing.

The third is responsiveness. I have a long-standing relationship with the head of sales at one of the major self-directed IRA custodians. He has a law degree, and we grab coffee whenever we have the chance. When I refer a client to him, he is responsive to that client. I have also seen custodians who are not responsive, where clients miss opportunities because they cannot get a callback or because the custodian takes too long to issue a check on a directed investment. You cannot operate in this space if you cannot move quickly. The custodian's responsiveness, on a real-world basis with a real client on the line, is one of the most reliable indicators of whether the relationship is going to work.

Checkbook IRAs

The self-directed IRA's gate fees and speed are the structural reasons the checkbook IRA has become popular. A checkbook IRA is an LLC owned one hundred percent by the IRA itself. Not by the natural person who is the IRA owner, but by the IRA. The LLC has its own bank account. The IRA owner serves as the manager of the LLC. The IRA, holding the membership interest, owns the LLC. The IRA owner, as manager, can sign checks on the LLC's account to fund investments without routing each transaction through the custodian and incurring a gate fee on every wire and expending precious time.

The structure is useful. It is also the most common place I see self-directed IRA owners get themselves into trouble. The checkbook LLC is an extension of the IRA. The same prohibited transaction rules apply to the LLC that apply to the IRA. There must be a tight firewall between the LLC's bank account and any other account the IRA owner controls. No commingling. No personal expenses paid from the LLC account, even temporarily. If you own a rental property in the LLC, you can't run out and grab paint from the hardware store using your personal credit card. No deposits from personal sources, even short-term loans the owner intends to repay. The owner manages the

LLC for the benefit of the IRA, and only for the benefit of the IRA. An IRA owner who treats the LLC's checking account as a convenient petty cash account has given the IRS the case the IRS needs to disqualify the entire IRA.

Years ago, when I was working at the bank, a client decided to roll an old 401(k) into a self-directed IRA to invest in real estate. He used the IRA to purchase a beach condo with the intent of renting it out as a short-term rental for tourists. That would have been fine. The problem started when he decided to renovate the unit. He paid for paint, flooring, appliances, furniture, and the other items you need to set up a short-term rental, all on his personal credit card. He did not understand that the IRS was going to read those personal credit card receipts as a contribution to the IRA. By paying for the renovation personally, he had effectively put money into the account outside the allowed contribution limits. The consequence was a disqualified IRA and a devastating taxable event on the full account balance. He had not stolen anything. He had simply paid for the paint from a prohibited source.

Construction Lending Inside a Self-Directed IRA

Construction lending is where the self-benefit analysis becomes most exposed. The construction loan involves draw requests, third-party inspections, mechanic's liens, change orders, contractor disputes, and a great deal of administrative work. An IRA owner who is also a contractor, or who is also a real estate operator with construction experience, will be tempted to take a hands-on role in administering the loan. That role, performed by the IRA owner, is the cleanest path to a self-benefit finding under audit. Think about it. You're providing valuable work which adds value to the property and, in turn, the IRA. That can be construed as a contribution.

The right structure is to keep the IRA owner out of the day-to-day work. The administration of the construction loan, the draw processing, the inspection coordination, and the document review should be with a third party engaged on arm's-length terms. The IRA pays the third party. The IRA owner does not step in and do it for free. The same logic applies to property preservation, contractor management, and any other operational activity on a construction loan held inside an IRA. This might be a gray area and there will be disagreement as to what exactly constitutes a contribution. If you have any doubt, I would err on the side of caution and not do what you're concerned about doing. At the very least, consult your attorney and tax advisor.

Subject-To Structures Inside an IRA

A subject-to structure, in which a property is acquired or financed with an existing mortgage left in place in the original borrower's name, carries elevated risk inside a self-directed IRA. The structure depends on the original mortgage remaining undisturbed while ownership and economic interest transfer. The IRA that becomes the beneficial owner of a property carrying an existing institutional mortgage in someone else's name is, at the same time, taking on the kind of structural complexity that the prohibited transaction rules were written to police. If you've heard me speak or read articles I've previously written, you probably know I'm not a fan of subject-to transactions. I'll try to leave my negative bias at the door for the rest of this discussion.

The exposures are several. The first is the standard due-on-sale clause in the underlying mortgage, which is not an IRA issue but is a transaction risk that does not disappear because the IRA is the new owner. The second is the question of whether the IRA owner, in negotiating the subject-to arrangement or in servicing the underlying mortgage from the IRA's side, is performing services for the benefit of the IRA in a way that the IRS would treat as self-benefit. The third is the question of whether the relationships among the IRA, the prior owner, and any servicing intermediary include disqualified-person interactions that the IRA owner has not analyzed. Subject-to inside an IRA is not widely understood in the IRA lending market. I would not run that structure without specific, written guidance from a qualified ERISA or tax practitioner who has reviewed the exact facts.

Owner-Occupied Residential Lending and the Personal Guaranty Problem

An IRA can lend on a wide range of collateral. When the IRA lends on owner-occupied residential property, two additional issues come into play. The first is licensing. A mortgage loan secured by owner-occupied residential property in most states requires the lender to hold the appropriate state license under the SAFE Act framework. The IRA's status as a retirement account does not exempt the loan from the licensing rule. The IRA owner who originates that loan personally, without a license, has a regulatory problem on top of any prohibited transaction problem.

The second is the personal guaranty issue we covered in Chapter 10 Part 1. A loan to an individual borrower secured by their primary residence is a consumer loan, and consumer loans on residential real estate have their own disclosure and underwriting framework. A loan to an entity that owns rental residential property is a business purpose loan, and a business purpose loan to an entity typically requires a personal guaranty from the principals of the entity. When the IRA is the lender, both of those structures have to be analyzed carefully. The IRA cannot accept a personal guaranty from a disqualified person to the IRA. The IRA cannot lend on terms that benefit the IRA owner outside the IRA. The standard small-balance owner-occupied loan structure that works for a non-IRA private lender does not always translate cleanly into an IRA-held loan.

Lending To an IRA, From the Other Side of the Table

Here is the part of the IRA lending market that is structurally favorable for the private lender who lends to other people's IRAs. Most institutional lenders will not lend to an IRA, or to an LLC owned by an IRA. The reason is recourse. In a standard business-purpose loan to an entity, the lender requires the natural-person owners of the entity to sign personal guaranties so that, in the event of default, the lender can pursue the guarantors as well as the entity. When the borrower is an IRA, or an LLC owned by an IRA, the IRA owner cannot provide a personal guaranty. To do so would be the IRA owner extending credit, indirectly, to their own IRA, which is a prohibited transaction and would bust the IRA. A handful of institutional lenders have built nonrecourse programs that lend to IRAs at lower leverage and a higher rate to compensate for the missing guaranty. Most institutional lenders will not engage at all.

A private lender who is willing to underwrite the IRA, the collateral, and the underlying borrower without recourse to a natural person can do real volume in this space. The pricing is higher than a conventional comparable loan. The leverage is lower. The underwriting has to be more rigorous because the lender's recovery is bounded by the collateral. The opportunity exists because the institutional lenders are absent. The framework does not change because the borrower is a retirement account. The Three C's apply. Character is the IRA's history of administration, the borrower's history of dealing with the IRA owner, and the operational track record of the deal sponsor. Capacity is the IRA's liquidity, the deal cash flow, and the reserve position the IRA can carry through a downturn. Collateral is the collateral. A private lender who knows what they are doing can underwrite this loan and price it properly. Without that experience, the lender will make a mistake the borrower's IRA pays for, and the borrower has limited ability to undo it.

Note Purchases Inside an IRA

The same rules apply to notes purchased inside an IRA, including seasoned paper bought at a discount. The IRA can buy a note from a non-disqualified seller. The IRA cannot buy a note that creates a creditor relationship between the IRA and a disqualified person. The IRA can hold the note through its term, accept the payments through the custodian or the checkbook LLC, and book the interest as ordinary income inside the IRA. The IRA cannot use that interest, or any portion of it, for the IRA owner's personal benefit outside the account.

The due diligence on a note acquisition for an IRA is the same due diligence we walked through in Chapter 10 Parts 1 and 2 and again in the workout chapters. The documentation has to be enforceable. The chain of assignments has to be complete. The insurance has to have the right mortgagee clause. The collateral has to support the position. Discount-priced paper carries the same enforceability questions whether the buyer is a personal account or a retirement account, and the IRA does not get a second chance at the due diligence after the trade closes.

A Word on UBIT and UDFI

One area I will not dwell on here, and it is a question for your tax professional, is Unrelated Business Income Tax and its cousin, Unrelated Debt-Financed Income. UBIT and UDFI are both real tax exposures for self-directed IRAs even though IRA income is normally tax deferred. UBIT shows up when the IRA's activity rises to the level of an ongoing trade or business. UDFI is the more common trap. It applies when the IRA borrows money to acquire or hold property, including a leveraged note purchase or a real estate acquisition financed with a nonrecourse loan, and it taxes the IRA on the share of income attributable to the borrowed money. Yes, my undergrad was in accounting, but that was a long, long time ago when dinosaurs roamed the Earth. That said, I know enough to know and admit that I do not know enough about either to advise on them. I will point them out here to make sure you ask your tax professional about both before you start lending or investing in real estate from your IRA.

The Underwriting Gap in IRA Lending

I regularly grab coffee with the head of sales for one of the better-known self-directed IRA custodians. He is a good guy, and we genuinely enjoy each other's perspective on the industry. The conversation moved one morning to the large number of his clients who lend money out of their IRAs without a clue what they are doing. His role prohibits him from providing investment advice, but he said that many of the loans those clients make leave him shaking his head. He and I went on to do an educational webinar together on the basics of private lending, centered on the Three C's of credit. The point of the webinar, and the point that belongs in this chapter as well, is that an IRA full of private loans is only as good as the underwriting that originated those loans. Many private lenders lend out of their IRAs. Few have the experience necessary to do it well, and fewer still understand the risk they are accepting.

Dougie Downer

I often say that you can't get a little bit pregnant. Either you are or you aren't. The IRA is either compliant or it is not. Mishandling an IRA can do a great deal of damage. There is no good-faith exception that makes the tax bill go away.

Chapter 19

The Performing Note Market and Re-Performance Pricing

In 2012 we were reviewing a potential portfolio purchase from a relatively new note seller out of New York. He was full of himself, and he did not really understand the credit side of what he was selling. He traded notes the way someone trades stocks or bonds. The credit aspect of the paper escaped him. The portfolio I was looking at was severely delinquent residential mortgage notes. There was little chance any of them would re-perform. Many of the collateral properties had been abandoned by the owners. They were zombie properties. Every one of the loans was upside down. The loan balance exceeded the value of the collateral on every position in the pool.

In a pool like that, the unpaid balance does not tell the buyer much about what the paper is worth. We priced the portfolio off the as-is value of the underlying collateral, with allowances for the cost and the time required to take each property back and dispose of it. The seller belittled us for that approach. He insisted we price off the UPB. We did not, and we could not come to terms on a price. As I have said before, you live to fight another day. I am not even sure if the seller is still in the business.

That story sets up the rest of this chapter. The unpaid balance is one input. It is not always the most important one, and on severely delinquent paper it is one of the least important. The price a buyer can responsibly pay for a note is bounded by what the note will actually produce, in real cash, under the conditions that actually exist.

There is a strong community of note investor educators in this country, built over decades by experienced practitioners who have spent careers in this market. This chapter does not duplicate their material and is not meant to. It is the credit perspective on the same pricing decision, written for the note investor at any point in their journey, whether you have been buying paper for many years or you are reading this before your first acquisition. The framework here complements the practitioner education already available to you and adds the underwriting analysis behind the math.

A performing note includes a borrower who is paying as agreed today. That is the only thing the word performing actually tells you. It does not tell you the borrower will continue to pay. It does not tell you the documentation is enforceable. It does not tell you the collateral is worth what the seller says it is. The credit risk on a performing note is the credit risk on the borrower, the file and documents, and the collateral. The price you pay for that paper is a function of how much of that risk you have actually verified.

This chapter is built around the math of pricing a note. Pricing is the question note investors ask more than any other, and the question they get the least direct answer on. The math is not difficult, but the framework can be, and the framework is where most note buyers run off the road. I am going to walk through, in real numbers, how we price a note at Castle Rock. The same math carries forward into Chapter 20, where we walk through nonperforming paper, because we price every note in two ways and the framework is the same in both cases. At this juncture, I'll point out that we're going to give you a very high-level view of how we price notes, but some of the nuances are proprietary to our company and how we do business.

Performing, Seasoned, and Current

The note market uses three terms that look interchangeable to the outsider and are not. Performing means the borrower is paying as agreed at the moment the seller is offering the note. Seasoned means the loan has a history of payments behind it, usually more than 12 months and often more than 24. Current means the loan is not delinquent right now.

Each of those signals something specific about borrower behavior, and each carries a different piece of risk information.

A performing note may have been performing for a single month. A note that paid for the first two years, slipped into delinquency, was modified, and is now paying again is also a performing note in the moment. It's known as "reperforming." The history determines what the word means in any given case.

A seasoned note has a longer track record, and the longer the track record, the more confidence most buyers place in the borrower's repayment behavior under the conditions that actually occurred. A note seasoned through a downturn is materially different from a note seasoned through nothing but a rising market. The word seasoned itself does not tell you which one you are buying. One personal note. I feel seasoning is over-relied upon in note circles. It's certainly not irrelevant. It's important, but many note buyers will completely ignore a newly originated loan that was thoroughly underwritten by a professional with documentation out the wazoo because it's not seasoned. My feelings on this subject might differ from others you've heard, but seasoning is not the end-all, be-all that many assign to it.

Current is the weakest of the three signals. A note that is current today may have been 30 days down last month, 60 days down the month before, and brought current with a one-time catch-up payment. The seller's offering memo will describe it as current. The collection notes will describe what actually happened. Read both and determine the reason and severity of the delinquency. You'll want to account for that in your decision to buy and the price you assign to that note.

UPB Is Not the Price

Most of the note industry prices everything on unpaid principal balance. The seller's offering memo leads with UPB. The pool data file, or "tape" as it's known in note circles, is organized by UPB. The bid is expressed as a percentage of UPB. 40 cents on the dollar means 40 cents on the unpaid principal balance. The convention is so embedded that the average buyer never thinks about whether UPB is the right input.

I am in the minority on this. UPB is one input. It is not the most important input, and on nonperforming paper, it is one of the least important inputs.

Consider a nonperforming loan that has not paid in 24 months and that owes you $200,000 on a property worth $150,000. If you foreclose, where is the additional $50,000 coming from? If the borrower had $50,000, they would likely be making their payments. You cannot get blood from a stone. The unpaid balance is a number on a screen. The recoverable cash is bounded by the collateral, the cost of recovery, and the time it takes to convert one to the other.

UPB matters in narrow ways. It tells you the size of the seller's exposure. It tells you the interest accrual you might inherit on a modification. On a performing loan, it tells you the principal stream the borrower is still scheduled to pay. It does not tell you what the loan is worth. Worth is a function of cash flow and risk. We price on cash flow and risk.

The Two Questions Every Note Buyer Should Ask

When I was a child, I was convinced I was going to hit the winning home run in Game 7 of the World Series to lift the St. Louis Cardinals to the championship. That did not work out. Life does not always go the way you plan. If every loan paid as agreed, there would be no nonperforming notes. There would only be performing ones.

That is the framing problem most note buyers carry into the deal. They look at a performing note and price it as if it will remain performing. They look at a nonperforming note and price it as if foreclosure will produce a specific number on a specific date. Both pricings depend on a single forecast of the future, and neither one applies when the future turns out differently.

We price every note in two ways. One price assumes the borrower pays as agreed. The other price assumes the borrower defaults at some point and we have to turn to the worst case scenario, which is taking the collateral back and disposing of it. We do not split the difference. We weight the two prices in our own way, but we tend to offer the lower of the two. The lower of the two has a name we use internally. We call it the strike price. The strike price is the highest amount we are willing to pay for the note.

The rest of this chapter is built around the math behind those two prices. Chapter 20 carries the math forward into nonperforming paper specifically. The framework is the same in both chapters. The variables change.

Backing Into the Parking Place

Before I work through the math, some context is important to understand. I do not price a note by guessing what it is worth and seeing if the yield is acceptable. I start with the yield I require, and I back into the price that produces that yield.

We call that backing into the parking place. The yield is the parking space. The price is how I steer to get there. You cannot just guess on a price to pay. You have to math the math. I know that is not proper grammar. I like it anyway.

The yield required is not a market number. It is an internal number set by the cost of capital, the risk class of the asset, the time required to manage the asset, and the alternatives sitting on the desk that morning. Two buyers looking at the same note will arrive at two different prices because their required yields are different, and the required yield is the variable that drives everything that follows.

When I see a note offered at a price, I do not start by asking whether the price looks fair. I start by asking what yield that price produces under the two scenarios. If the answer is below my required yield in either scenario, the price is wrong. The note may still be worth buying, but at a different number.

The Math of Pricing a Performing Note

A performing note is, at its core, a stream of monthly payments running until maturity. From the buyer's perspective, the buyer pays cash today and receives that monthly stream over time. The math the buyer uses to value the stream is the same math a fixed-income desk at a stock brokerage uses to value a bond, and the bond pricing function on a financial calculator that handles a bond will handle a fully amortizing note without issue.

For a finance person who started in the business more than twenty years ago, if you did not go through more than two HP 12-C calculators in your career, you were not a finance pro. We used them constantly for amortization schedules, monthly payments, internal rates of return, and exactly the kind of discount calculation we are about to run. The 12-C is still produced. The math has not changed.

Let me work an example. A performing first-lien loan with a remaining balance of $100,000, a note rate of 7%, and 7 years remaining on what was originally a 15-year fully amortizing schedule. The buyer's required yield is 15%.

The first step is the monthly payment. The contract says the loan was a 15-year fully amortizing structure at 7%. The current balance of $100,000 with 7 years remaining at the contract rate produces a monthly payment that fully amortizes the balance over the remaining term. The calculator inputs are n at 84 months, "i" at 0.5833% per month (the contract rate of 7% divided by 12), PV at $100,000, and FV at 0. Solve for PMT.

The answer is approximately $1,509.27 per month. That is the payment the borrower is making, and that is the cash flow stream the buyer is acquiring.

The second step is the present value at the buyer's required yield. The buyer does not want to earn the contract rate of 7%. The buyer wants to earn the 15% yield they steer toward when they back into the price. How do you calculate this if the borrower is paying a payment based on 7%, but the note buyer wants to yield 15%? You discount the note when you buy it. The calculator inputs change. n stays at 84 months. "i" (interest, not "i" as in me...that was confusing as I wrote it) changes to 1.25% per month, which is the required yield of 15% divided by 12. PMT stays at $1,509.27. FV stays at 0, because the note fully amortizes. Solve for PV.

The answer is approximately $78,214.

That is the price the buyer pays today to receive a 15% annualized yield on a fully amortizing 7-year stream of payments from a borrower paying as agreed. The discount to UPB is approximately $21,786, or 21.8%. In market shorthand, the note prices at 78 cents on the dollar.

A few things to notice in that example.

The buyer does not earn the 7% contract rate. The buyer earns the 15% yield the buyer required when they set the price. The 7% is the math that ties the borrower's payment to the borrower's balance. The 15% is the math that ties the buyer's cash today to the buyer's cash flow over time.

The discount exists because the required yield is higher than the contract rate. If the required yield equaled the contract rate, the note would price at par, meaning the buyer would pay 100% of UPB. If the required yield were lower than the contract rate, the note would trade at a premium, meaning the buyer would pay more than UPB. The private note market is built around discounts because the typical required yield on private paper is materially higher than the contract rate at origination.

If the loan has a balloon at maturity rather than full amortization, the calculator inputs change in one place. FV is no longer zero. FV is the balloon balance at the maturity date. The buyer is now valuing two streams at once, the monthly payments through the balloon date and the lump-sum balloon at the end. The math handles both without breaking a sweat.

Now, here's where your portfolio gets a major boost. What happens if the note pays off early? Good for you! You want that! That discount you received when purchasing the note gets "compressed" into the shorter time frame and your annualized yield, as a result, shoots through the roof. Let's say our same example pays off in 3 years versus the planned 7. Your yield is much, much more than 15%. Kudos to you! We'll discuss this more when we get to "Yield to Call."

The Math When the Borrower Does Not Pay

Now take the same loan and re-price it under the assumption that the borrower stops paying and we turn to the collateral.

The variables change. We are no longer valuing a stream of monthly payments. We are valuing a single lump sum that arrives at the end of a recovery timeline, net of the costs of getting there.

Assume the collateral is currently worth $95,000. Assume the buyer's estimate of total collection and legal costs to foreclose and dispose of the property is $5,000. Assume the timeline from purchase to disposition is 18 months. Assume the buyer's required yield remains 15%.

The net proceeds at disposition are $90,000. That is the $95,000 collateral value minus the $5,000 in costs.

The calculator inputs are n at 18 months, "i" at 1.25% per month, PMT at 0 (no payments are coming in during the recovery period because the loan is nonperforming), FV at $90,000, and solve for PV.

The answer is approximately $71,967.

That is the price the buyer pays today to receive a 15% annualized yield from a single lump sum 18 months in the future, with no intervening cash flow. The discount to UPB is approximately $28,033, or 28%. In market shorthand, the note prices at 72 cents on the dollar.

Now compare the two prices.

The performing scenario produces a price of approximately $78,214.

The nonperforming scenario produces a price of approximately $71,967.

The lower of the two is $71,967. That is usually our strike price on this loan. That is the highest amount we are willing to pay for it. If we have a strong view that the loan will continue performing, we may weight the price upward toward the $78,000 number. We tend to offer nearer to the lower of the two but we do use our judgement. The strike price gives us a margin for being wrong about which scenario plays out.

The Strike Price and Why the Lower Number Wins

The strike price is the protection against being wrong about the future.

The buyer who pays $78,000 on the assumption that the loan continues performing is, when the borrower stops paying, sitting on a recovery that is valued at $72,000. The buyer has paid roughly $6,000 more than the asset is worth in the scenario that actually came true. That loss is the difference between two pricings the buyer could have run at the front end and chose not to.

The buyer who pays $72,000 on the strike price approach is sitting on a recovery that hits the price they paid if a borrower defaults. The buyer is now whole. The buyer is also whole, with upside, if the loan continues performing, because the cash flow at the contract terms over a discounted entry point produces a yield above the buyer's required 15%.

The strike price is not the only price a buyer can pay. There are sellers who will not take the lower number, and there are buyers willing to weight the performing case more heavily because the information gleaned from their due diligence supports it. The point is that the strike price is the base, hard number. The buyer who has not run both pricings does not know where the strike price is, and therefore does not know how much room they are giving up when they pay above it.

The Circus Whip

There is a useful image for what happens to a discount as the remaining term changes.

Think of a circus whip. If you flick your wrist at the handle, the movement is small and slow. The farther you go out along the whip, the larger and faster the movement gets, until the tip cracks faster than the speed of sound. Seven hundred and sixty-one miles an hour at the tip from an inch of motion at the handle, producing a small sonic boom.

The same effect runs through note pricing. A small change in the yield you require, applied over a long remaining term, produces a large change in the price you pay. A small error in the timeline you assume for a nonperforming workout, applied to a long recovery period, produces a large error in the price the math says you should pay.

The same logic applies to driving down a highway. A small steering correction at sixty miles an hour, held for a long distance, takes you onto a different road than the one you started on. The further you travel, the more you veer off course.

The practical takeaway is two-part. The first is that the further out maturity sits, the greater the discount required to produce a given yield, and the more sensitive the answer is to the inputs. The second is that the inputs themselves have to be the right inputs. A loan with 18 years to maturity priced at a yield that is wrong by even 1% produces a different price than the same loan priced correctly, and the difference compounds out the length of the stream. Pay attention to the variables in the calculation. Small errors at the wrist become large misses at the tip.

Yield to Maturity Versus Yield to Call

The two yield concepts the note buyer needs to keep separate are yield to maturity and yield to call.

Yield to maturity is the yield the buyer earns if the loan runs to its scheduled end. Every payment is made exactly on time. The final payment pays off the balance. The calculator inputs and the price walk through the example earlier in this chapter. Keep in mind that this, in practice, never happens. Remember our earlier example of the car and the slight change in steering veering you off course. Payments made early or late will alter the yield to maturity in the same way.

Yield to call is the yield the buyer earns if the loan prepays. The borrower refinances at month 30. The loan is gone. The remaining stream of monthly payments the buyer was counting on does not arrive. The buyer received a partial stream and the principal payoff at month thirty, and the yield on the actual cash flow is calculated against the price the buyer paid. By the way, congratulations if this happens. You just made a higher yield based on your discount. If you paid a premium, oops! You took a hit.

The difference between the two yields is important because a note bought at a deep discount produces a higher yield to call than to maturity. The borrower paying off early returns the principal sooner, and the discount the buyer captured on the principal is realized faster, which raises the annualized return. A note bought at a premium produces a lower yield to call than to maturity. The premium the buyer paid is amortized over fewer payments than expected, and the early payoff returns less than the buyer anticipated.

A disciplined note buyer prices to both yields and accepts the worse of the two. If the loan is going to prepay, the buyer wants to be paid for that. If the loan is going to run to term, the buyer wants to be paid for that. Pricing to whichever yield is more favorable to the seller and assuming the borrower will accommodate is not pricing. It is hoping.

Prepayment Speed Assumptions

The institutional market uses a metric called CPR, conditional prepayment rate, to model how fast a pool of loans is expected to pay off. The CPR is an annualized estimate of the percentage of the remaining balance that will prepay in a given year. It also depends on the law of large numbers in a similar way that insurance companies price life insurance. They cannot tell you exactly when Doug Smith will die. If they take ten thousand people of the same age, diet, smoking habits, drinking habits, and health, they can be pretty accurate on the average age of those ten thousand at the time of their passing. They win some and they lose some, but the law of large numbers says that the more samples in the pool and the more historical data they have on like samples, the more accurate the average becomes.

Private paper does not move with the precision of institutional pools, but the underlying logic still applies. Higher-rate paper prepays faster when rates fall. Lower-rate paper prepays slower under the same conditions. Borrowers with strong credit prepay faster than borrowers with weak credit, because the strong credits have refinancing options the weak credits do not. Owner-occupied loans prepay faster than investor loans, because owner-occupied borrowers respond to consumer mortgage advertising. Investor loans prepay on schedules driven by the property's business plan rather than by rate moves.

A note buyer who assumes a long average life on paper that is going to prepay quickly will overpay. The pricing math runs out to the original maturity, the actual cash flow usually ends earlier, and the realized yield is the yield to call rather than the yield to maturity the buyer modeled at the front end.

The Seller's Pricing Model

Although many sellers auction off notes they wish to sell, some sellers offer notes with a price already attached. The price comes from the seller's model. The model carries the seller's assumptions about cash flow timing, recovery rates, and yield. None of those assumptions are the buyer's assumptions.

A pricing model produced by a seller is a sales document. It is not a piece of due diligence. The buyer who accepts the seller's model and prices off of it has outsourced the most important decision in the transaction to the party with the strongest incentive to land a high number.

Run your own model. The math is not overly complicated once you understand it. The calculator inputs are the same ones we have already walked through. The variables are yours to set, and they should reflect your required yield, your timeline assumptions, your recovery cost estimates, and your read on the borrower's behavior. The seller's model is useful as a comparison point and as a window into how the seller is thinking. It is not your strike price.

Pool Due Diligence on a Multi-Asset Acquisition

When the buyer is acquiring a pool of notes, the due diligence is structured around the loan-level data file the seller provides. The industry term for that file is the tape, and the tape is the foundation of the bid.

The tape is a spreadsheet, usually delivered in Excel format, with one row per loan and columns for the variables the buyer supposedly needs to price the pool. The standard columns include the loan number, the borrower's name, the property address, the original loan amount, the unpaid principal balance, the note rate, the original term, the maturity date, the current monthly payment, the next payment due date, the current escrow balance, the credit score at origination, and a payment history grid showing performance over the most recent 12 to 24 months.

The tape is the loan as it sits on the seller's books. The actual loan files contain everything else. Whether the original note is in the file, whether the chain of assignments is complete, whether the title policy is current, whether the property is insured, whether the borrower's contact information is still good, none of that is in the tape. The tape itself is also usually an optimistic view of the portfolio. The data is likely factual on its own terms, but it is still information you have to interpret and verify before you can responsibly price the pool.

The due diligence pass on a pool acquisition starts with the tape and ends with the loan files themselves. A sample of files is pulled, the sample is read against the tape, and the discrepancies are catalogued. A pool where the sample reveals 5% missing notes, 10% gaps in the assignment chain, and 20% stale insurance is a pool that prices differently from one where the sample seems complete and accurate. The buyer who skips the file review and prices off the tape alone is buying the seller's documentation risk along with the loans, at the seller's price. If you fail to do your due diligence, you probably deserve to lose a few bucks.

Single-Asset Due Diligence

On a single-asset note purchase, the same process runs at smaller scale. The loan file is the primary source of information. The buyer reads the original note, the recorded mortgage or deed of trust, the title policy, the insurance binder, the assignment chain, the collection notes, and the payment history.

The single-asset due diligence pass is also where most enforceability problems get caught. The note is missing. The notary stamp is illegible. The assignment to the seller was never recorded. The property has a junior lien the seller did not disclose. Every one of those facts changes the price and even the buying decision, and every one of them is sitting in the file waiting to be found.

Documentation Review on Performing Paper

A hard situation on a performing note is when you discover an enforceability problem on a loan that is paying as agreed.

The temptation is to ignore it. The borrower is paying. The buyer is collecting. The hole in the file has not surfaced yet. Why move on it?

The reason to move on it is that the value of a performing note is the cash flow plus the option to enforce it. The option to enforce is what gives the cash flow its floor. A note with a hole in the documentation has no floor. When and if the borrower stops paying, the hole comes to the forefront, and the loss mitigation negotiation begins from a position the note buyer likely cannot win.

The right response is to identify the problem, document it in the file, and pursue the remedy that is still available. A missing assignment can be cured by a corrective assignment from the prior seller. A notarization defect on the mortgage can sometimes be cured by a reformation action or by a fresh signing if the borrower will cooperate. A missing original note may have a copy on file and a lost note affidavit available. None of those remedies are easy or quick. All of them are easier and quicker before the borrower stops paying than after.

We covered the underlying document set in Chapter 10 Parts 1 and 2. The due diligence at acquisition is the same documentary checklist, applied as a buyer rather than as an originator. The remedies, where they exist, are in the same body of state law and require the same competent attorney to execute.

The Memo at Acquisition

We walked through the LOM and the credit memo in Chapter 12 as origination tools. The same framework applies at acquisition.

The LOM at acquisition documents the loan being acquired, the due diligence performed, the conclusions reached, the price calculated under each of the two scenarios, the strike price selected, the discount to UPB, the yield projected to maturity, the yield projected to call, the prepayment assumption used, the recovery timeline assumed, the recovery costs assumed, and the file conditions identified that have to be cured before or after closing.

The acquisition LOM is the record of what was actually approved, on what facts, at what price. It is the document the buyer reads sometime later when the loan is in workout, and it is the document the buyer's counsel reads when the loan is in litigation. It is also the document the buyer reads against the seller's representations when a piece of the file later turns out to be different from what the seller said it was.

A buyer who acquires notes without writing a memo is buying without writing down the basis for the bid. That is the same position the lender takes when they fund a loan without an LOM. It is a problem of laying out your reasoning for the buy, of accountability, and of audit, and it is solved the same way, by writing the memo at the time the decision is made.

Servicing Transfer at Acquisition

We walked through servicing in Chapter 13 as a continuous operational function. The transfer of servicing at acquisition is where most of the value documented in the file is either preserved or quietly given away.

The records that have to move with the loan include the original note with its endorsement chain, the recorded mortgage or deed of trust with the complete chain of recorded assignments, the title policy, the insurance binders or declarations pages, the closing file, the most recent payment history, the most recent borrower contact information, the most recent tax and escrow information, any active modification or forbearance agreements, the collection notes from the prior servicer, and any open work items the prior servicer was handling. The handoff has to be complete when the new servicer boards the loan. Anything missing at that time tends to stay missing.

The boarding process at the new servicer is where the data file from the seller is reconciled against the actual loan records. The borrower's contact information is verified. The next payment due date is confirmed. Any payment in transit is identified. The escrow balance is reconciled. The taxes and insurance are confirmed in force. The introduction letter to the borrower is sent, identifying the new servicer, the new payment address, and the customer service contact. None of that is difficult, but all of it has to happen, and the buyer who outsources servicing without confirming that it happened on every loan in the pool ends up with collection problems down the road that trace back to a boarding issue out of the gate.

The Forward Reference to Chapter 20

We have walked through pricing a note in two ways in this chapter. The performing case and the nonperforming case. In our shop, the strike price is usually the lower of the two.

Chapter 20 carries the math forward into a pool of nonperforming loans. The variables shift, but the pricing logic is the same. We start with the yield we require, and we back into the price under each scenario. We pick the lower price. We document the basis for the bid before we agree to a buy.

Dougie Downer

A performing note is a borrower paying as agreed today. The discount you paid is not the margin of safety you think it is unless the documentation, the collateral, and the servicing all support the same conclusion.

Chapter 20

Nonperforming Notes and Workout Acquisitions

Buying nonperforming loans, for me, was really an offshoot of my days as a banker when I handled special assets for a community bank. I had been a lender for about 18 years prior to directly working on larger commercial "bad loans." Before that, I was aware that loans could be sold, but it never occurred to me that there was an entire industry surrounding the buying and selling of nonperforming loans. During the crash of 2007 and 2008, I dove in headfirst and used what I had learned over a long formal credit career to build very profitable portfolios of nonperforming loans for us and our investor clients.

The discount on a nonperforming note is not a bargain. It is a price the seller is paying you to take a problem off their hands. Whether you make money on the trade depends entirely on whether you can solve the problem...and how you price it. The saying "you make your money on the buy" holds just as true in nonperforming loans as it does in real estate. People who can solve problems earn a profit. People who cannot end up holding the problem and the discount turns into a loss.

We covered the math in Chapter 19. The dual-pricing approach and the strike price discussion can be found there, and I am not going to walk you through that again. Flip back if you need the calculator inputs or the worked example. This chapter starts once you close on the nonperforming loan.

The Nonperforming Data File

When a seller offers a pool, they typically send a tape. On nonperforming paper, the tapes are a bit different because the loans are already in default. What you get from the tape is the seller's view of the loan. The borrower's view is not in it, and the borrower's view is the one that will determine how we resolve the loan. A borrower who stopped paying because they lost a job has a very different conversation ahead of them than a borrower who decided the property was no longer worth holding. That distinction is not in the tape. You will find it in the collection notes. Read them carefully.

There is one piece of information missing from the tape, and I want to point it out up front. Property condition on a nonperforming loan can deteriorate fast. A loan that stopped paying several months ago has spent that time without insurance monitoring, without exterior maintenance, and in many cases without occupancy. The original property value carried on the tape is the value at origination. Nobody at the seller has typically been inside that house since the borrower stopped paying. Assume the property is in worse shape than that original valuation until someone you trust has visited it.

UPB Versus Collateral Value

I said in Chapter 19 that the industry leans on UPB way too hard, and that the bias is most pronounced on nonperforming paper. That view does not change here. Chapter 19 walked through the math. This chapter walks through the inputs that drive the math. The collateral value, the recovery cost, the workout timeline, and the resolution path are four variables that move the strike price up or down. Getting those four variables right is what makes your pricing more accurate.

On a nonperforming loan with $200,000 owed and a property worth $150,000, the foreclosure does not magically produce the missing $50,000. We covered the blood-from-a-stone problem in Chapter 19 and there is no reason to belabor it. The point I want to hit home here is that on nonperforming paper, the collateral, the cost of getting to the collateral, and the speed at which you can do it matter far more than the UPB figure.

Due Diligence Before the Bid

Nonperforming due diligence is more difficult than performing due diligence for one reason. The loan is already in default. Anything in the file I cannot independently verify, I am buying on faith. I do not buy anything on trust.

I read the collection notes first. I want to know whether the borrower has been talking to anybody. Are they returning calls? Have they offered to pay something? Have they asked for a modification? Have they offered to surrender the property? Have they retained counsel? I find the answers in the collection notes. From them I can see what kind of file I have. If the borrower has been negotiating with the prior servicer for six months, I have a workout. If the borrower has gone dark for two years, I have a foreclosure or a skip trace ahead of me.

I send somebody to look at the property. This is the same point I made in Chapter 17 about BPOs, and it gets more urgent on nonperforming collateral. I want a local contractor or trusted agent walking the perimeter, taking current photos, and giving me a short condition report. That report drives the recovery side of the strike price. A desk-produced BPO on a nonperforming property is almost worthless in my humble opinion.

I pull the title and the assignment chain. We covered the assignment of mortgage and the allonge in Chapter 10 Part 2. On nonperforming paper, the assignment chain is where many of the enforceability problems hide. The original mortgage was recorded. The loan was sold once or twice. The recording on one of those assignments never happened. The public record shows the wrong holder. I am about to bid on a loan I will have to perfect before I can enforce, and the cost of that perfection has to come out of my price.

I confirm the original note. The traditional rule is that the holder of the endorsed original note enforces it. That rule is not gone, but several jurisdictions have softened it in practice. Courts have grown more willing to credit a properly executed lost note affidavit, supported by credible secondary evidence, where the missing original existed and was properly endorsed. I still want to know where the original is. I just no longer treat a missing original as automatically fatal the way I once did. The cost of perfection varies by jurisdiction. I build the cost into my bid.

Finally, I look at what workout options are actually still available given everything I just read. A loan with a complete file and an engaged borrower offers paths a loan with a defective assignment and a missing borrower does not. The price gap between those two acquisitions is the difference in operational cost to get to a resolution.

The Resolution Toolkit, In Order of Preference

The resolution paths I reach for on nonperforming acquisitions are the same paths we discussed in Chapter 16 in the workout context. The order I prefer them in is different from a portfolio lender's order, because I set my price ahead of time on the assumption the loan would resolve one way or another. The order below is mine. I will tell you why I prefer each one.

Re-Performance Through Workout

The best outcome is to get the borrower paying again. Re-performance pays me back through the cash flow stream rather than through the collateral. The discount I captured at acquisition compresses into a higher realized yield because the cash flow is now coming in at the contract rate against my lower cost basis. The property stays where it is. I never have to take possession.

Re-performance only works when the borrower is both willing to pay and able to pay under terms I can live with. Ability comes from the borrower's actual financial situation, which I get by asking and verifying. Willing without able does not produce a re-performance. Able without willing produces a fight. I have spent more months than I care to admit on files where I confused one for the other. There is a difference between "can't" and "won't."

Re-performance is not a portfolio strategy. It is a result that comes out of the conversation with each individual borrower. The buyer who walks into the acquisition assuming every loan in the pool will re-perform has built a plan that will not succeed. Some loans re-perform. Identifying which ones is not something the tape can do. You learn that from your careful due diligence and client conversations.

Deed in Lieu of Foreclosure

If re-performance is off the table, the next path I want to follow is a deed in lieu of foreclosure. We covered the mechanics in Chapter 16 and again in Chapter 17. A deed in lieu returns the collateral to me in weeks rather than months, saves the legal cost of a contested foreclosure, and saves every dollar of carrying cost between today and the day the foreclosure would have closed.

I have had a lot of success on deeds in lieu, and the path is almost always the same. I get the borrower on the phone. I treat them with respect. I say "Tell me your situation" with empathy, and then I shut up and listen. Don't talk. Listen. The big lenders and big servicers often do not have this conversation. They are trained to wring the recovery on every file, not to find the fastest resolution that serves both parties. As an independent note buyer I have the room to operate differently, and the yield on a loan resolved through a deed in lieu quickly is materially better than the yield on the same loan resolved through a foreclosure many months later. Chapter 19 demonstrated that point in real numbers.

On the structure, I use the one I described in Chapter 17. I waive the deficiency in exchange for the property in broom-swept condition and a clean signing. The borrower walks away with their credit less damaged, with closure on the obligation, and without the expense and indignity of being sued. I walk away with the collateral cleanly, on a timeline that protects the yield.

A different angle the industry takes is what is called cash for keys. The buyer pays the borrower a cash amount to leave the property in exchange for the deed and a clean handover. I have been asked to do that more times than I can count. I have never once done it, and I do not intend to. The reason is principle. The day I write the first cash for keys check is the day I lose the ability to look the next borrower in the eye and say I do not do that. I do not want to compete with the borrower's perception of what their cooperation is worth. I want to compete on the real value the deed in lieu carries for them.

That real value, in my experience, is the credit protection. A borrower several months delinquent already has a damaged credit profile and is trying to keep it from getting worse. The waiver of the deficiency, combined with the avoidance of a foreclosure on the credit file, is substantially more valuable to most borrowers than the cost of a moving van. The numbers favor the structure without cash. Our results consistently bear that out.

Note Resale

A nonperforming note that is not resolving cleanly, and that I do not want to push through foreclosure, can be sold to another buyer. Many times, it's because it's in an area that I don't have experience in and don't have great boots on the ground. The market for nonperforming paper is active and there is almost always a bid on the other side of the trade, even for difficult files. The price will reflect the difficulty, which usually means selling at a discount to my cost basis. If I bought the loan at a strike price below the worst-case scenario, I can usually resell at a price that returns most if not all of my capital and frees up my asset management attention for files that are working. More often than not, we make money on the deal.

Note resale is a legitimate exit. It is not a failure. I bought the loan in good faith, ran the workout, and concluded that the resolution path through my shop was longer or harder than the discount was paying me for. Clearing the position and moving on is the right call. We talked about this in Chapter 17 when we walked through cases where it does not pay to complete a foreclosure. Pursuing a recovery whose cost exceeds the recovery is stubbornness. Passing the file to a buyer better equipped to operate it is operational good sense.

Modification

Modification is the path I reach for the least, and I want to explain why.

A modification permanently changes the contract. The interest rate, the payment, the maturity date, or some combination is rewritten. My pricing math at acquisition was built around the original contract. When I modify, I am rebuilding the cash flow stream on terms less favorable to me. Unless the modified stream is one the borrower can actually sustain and produces a yield at or above my required yield on the new basis, I have converted a nonperforming loan into a slowly performing loan that will re-default in a year.

There is a place for modification. A borrower with a short-term hardship, a stable repayment ability on the other side of the hardship, and a sincere willingness to commit to the new structure can be modified successfully. The condition is that I have actually verified the hardship, the post-hardship ability, and the willingness, and that I have run the pricing math on the modified terms before I sign anything. A modification offered to make a nonperforming loan look performing on the books is not a workout. It is kicking the can down the road.

Foreclosure

We covered foreclosure mechanics in Chapter 17 and bankruptcy procedure in Chapter 16. There is no reason to repeat any of that. The foreclosure path on a nonperforming acquisition is the path I take when every other path has been considered, declined, or deemed unworkable. The strike price I paid assumed this path was on the table. The operational effort between acquisition and the sheriff's sale is what the discount was paying me for.

One operational point worth covering here. Time really erodes yield. The math in Chapter 19 demonstrated how a longer recovery timeline compresses the annualized return. The attorney handling the foreclosure is the single largest lever I have on how fast the timeline runs, and therefore on what the yield turns out to be.

I have used two kinds of foreclosure attorney over the years. The first kind is out of the office a lot, slow to return calls, slow to file responses, willing to accept opposing counsel's continuances without pushback, and prone to letting deadlines slip. The second kind sends each required notice the day after the previous notice expires, returns calls inside the same business day, files motions early, and pushes the calendar at the pace the law allows. On two identical files in the same jurisdiction, the second attorney produces a materially better yield than the first. Same law, same loan, same borrower behavior. Different timing.

Find the foreclosure attorneys who do the job well. Pay them on time. Give them what they ask for promptly. Then let them work the way they know how to work. The relationship pays for itself many times over.

The Borrower Conversation After Acquisition

The single most undervalued tool I have on a nonperforming file is the conversation with the borrower.

Before I make the call, I read the file, the collection notes from the prior servicer, the original underwriting information where I have it, the loan history, the modification history, the default notices, and any letters the borrower sent. The point of the reading is to walk into the call knowing more than the borrower expects me to know. The point is also to walk in with a basic feel for what the borrower is actually dealing with.

The opening of the call is the introduction. I identify myself as the new note holder. I am not the prior servicer. I am not the foreclosure attorney. I am the new owner of the note, and I am calling to introduce myself and to understand their situation.

The middle of the call is the borrower speaking. I ask about their situation, then I shut up and listen. The borrower will tell me most of what I need to know if I give them the room to do it. They will tell me whether they want to stay in the property. They will tell me whether they can afford a payment, and what payment they could realistically handle. They will tell me whether they have already decided to walk away from the property. They will tell me whether they are angry, frightened, embarrassed, or some combination of all three. Everything I need to resolve the file is there if you shut up and listen. Fight the temptation to talk and interrupt. Listen.

We then have to decide what kind of conversation to have. A borrower who wants to stay and can carry a modified payment gets a modification conversation. A borrower who wants to walk away gets a deed in lieu conversation. A borrower who is paralyzed gets time and a scheduled callback. The note buyer who walks in with a single offer and presses it regardless of what the borrower says has wasted the call and not listened at all.

Tone matters more on these calls than people who have not made them realize. Speak with empathy. Speak in a friendly, non-threatening way. Never threaten. Treat the borrower like a person with dignity, because they are. They are almost certainly dealing with more in their life than the loan you are calling about. Many of the people I work with come from many different religions, and most religions teach some version of mercy. One of the key concepts of my own religion and belief system is, "Blessed are the merciful, for they shall receive mercy." That verse belongs in collection calling. You catch more flies with honey than with vinegar, and a borrower who feels you care will pick up the phone the next time you call. You can't fake empathy. If you don't really mean it, have someone who does handle the client contact.

I learned that lesson once from the wrong side of the table. I had thought I had paid a bill that I had not. The collection agent who called treated me like a deadbeat criminal for being a couple of days late on a payment I genuinely believed I had made. At first I was embarrassed.

Then thirty-five years of credit experience kicked in. I realized I was just one number on his call list, and that his behavior had nothing to do with me. I asked him if he was having a bad day. He hung up on me. I then called my former coworker, a friend who was the commercial bank executive on my account, apologized for the error, and asked him to move money from another account to cover the bill. His answer was, "No problem, dude. I got you." I never mentioned the collection agent to my banker buddy.

The lesson is direct. Treat people with dignity, respect, and grace. If they are behind on a payment, they are likely dealing with more than the one thing you are calling about. Do not come at them like a spider monkey. Show genuine care. Ask about their situation, then shut up and listen. You will find that solutions get easier when there is an open line of communication, and that borrowers will not duck you when they believe you actually care. Both sides come out better.

When the Borrower Cannot Be Found

Some borrowers cannot be reached by ordinary means. They have changed phones. They have moved. They have stopped opening mail. The prior servicer's last good number is six months stale. The conversation I just described cannot happen if the borrower will not pick up.

My first stop is the prior servicer's full file, including the collection notes, the most recent contact attempts, any emergency contacts, and any cosigner information. My second stop is the public record. Property tax records, court filings, corporate registrations, anywhere the borrower has been visible. My third stop, more and more often, is social media.

We had a foreclosure not long ago where we could not get the husband and wife served. They were ducking us. They were in the middle of a divorce. The husband had quit his job and we had no current employer for service. The wife had moved out and was not returning calls. Service was at a complete stop. Then the husband posted on his personal

Facebook page about his great new job, named the company, and mentioned the shift he worked. The wife posted on her own personal Facebook page about the new love of her life, with photos, tagged in a relationship status. The new boyfriend had an unusual name. We looked him up in the county property appraiser's records and found his address. Service was easy after that.

The point of the story is not that social media solves every skip trace. The point is that borrowers regularly tell the world online exactly where they are and what they are doing, and the information is free to anybody who looks. Studying a borrower's social media also gives you a window into their situation and their motivations. Spend the time learning who the borrower is before you reach for a generic script. A call that lands with some understanding of the borrower's actual life sounds very different from a call that opens with a loan number.

Earning the Discount

Re-performance is often a result of your working with the borrower in an empathetic manner. The note buyer who priced the discount on acquisition and then sat back waiting for the resolution to happen on its own has paid full price for the asset, whether they realized it or not. You have to put in the effort and do it in a professional manner in order to hit your yield targets.

A note buyer with the operational capacity to do that, or with a team built to do it, earns the discount. Without that capacity or team, the buyer has paid for an asset class whose returns require effort and never supplied the effort. The result is predictable. The file ages. The discount erodes. The borrower's situation deteriorates. The recovery comes in below the buyer's required yield. The discount captured at acquisition was the seller's payment for effort the buyer never expended.

Dougie Downer

Resist the temptation to treat delinquent borrowers poorly. You have no idea what is happening in their lives, and it is likely that they are struggling in many aspects of their life if they are past due on your loan. Show grace, mercy, and compassion. Show a willingness not to judge, but to understand and come to a reasonable solution for the portfolio and the borrower.

Chapter 21

Private Lending Funds: Where Capital Becomes a Credit System

A private lending fund is a small bank with no charter, no examiners, and one manager who answers for every credit decision. When the manager calls a loan right, the pool earns. When the manager calls a loan wrong, the pool eats the loss across every investor at once. Pooled capital multiplies the manager's judgment in both directions. I have run small funds for a long time, and I have made nearly every mistake that can be made running one. The mistakes are also the most useful part of this chapter. Theory does not teach this part of the business. The mistakes do.

The community of private lending educators has built a substantial body of material on fund setup, capital raising, investor relations, and the broader operating playbook. This chapter does not duplicate that work and is not meant to. It is the credit perspective on what the manager does with the capital once the raise is done, written for the manager at any point in their fund journey, whether you are building your first pool or you have run several over multiple cycles. The framework here complements the practitioner material already available to you and adds the credit officer's view of the operating decisions the manager makes day to day.

The Year I Was Spartacus

The biggest mistake I made the first year I managed a pool was that I did too well. As the end of the year approached, I went looking for ways to squeeze more return out of the portfolio. We posted our numbers, and I stood up on the table like a dominant gorilla thumping my chest and announced that I was Spartacus.

The next year the returns were still massive. Not as high as the year before, but still through the roof. All I heard from investors was, why weren't the returns as high as last year. The numbers were still excellent. The numbers also did not match the expectation I had set with my chest-thumping. The lesson was as direct as it sounds. Manage the expectations you set. People selectively hear what they want to hear. They hear what you led them to believe last time. Set the bar at the moon and anything below the moon gets read as a disappointment, no matter how good the actual number is.

PPMs, Reg D, and the Cost of Setup

Setting up a private lending fund is not free. The legal work to draft a private placement memorandum, the subscription documents, the operating agreement, the investor questionnaires, and the rest of the package will run into the thousands of dollars before you have raised a single dollar of capital. We paid that bill the first time, the right way, with a securities attorney who knew the territory. I would not recommend going any other route. The cost of the setup is small compared to the cost of doing it badly and finding out under a regulator's questioning that your offering was defective.

Regulation D is the federal exemption most small private lending funds operate under. The two rules most relevant are Rule 506(b) and Rule 506(c), each with its own rules on general solicitation and accredited investor verification. The practical limit of Reg D for a small fund is that the universe of investors you can accept money from is restricted to accredited investors in most structures, and the verification requirements on Rule 506(c) in particular take real work on every subscription. Know who your investors are, document that they qualify, and keep the records the regulator may someday ask about. The lawyer drafts the package. The manager has to operate it.

A Note on Capital Raising

Capital raising is a different skill set than credit underwriting or portfolio management. A strong credit officer can still struggle to translate the underwriting language into a vocabulary that lands with non-credit investors. Some managers are naturals at the raise. Others are not. If you are not, hire or partner with someone who is. The fund cannot exist without the capital, and the capital does not show up just because your credit skill set is good.

Capital and Deal Flow

The hardest balancing act in running a fund is keeping the capital and the deal flow in proportion. Too little capital and the deals you have committed to will not get funded on time, and your referral sources will quietly route their next deal somewhere else. Too much capital and the idle balances sitting in the operating account earn nothing while the investors are expecting a yield on every dollar of their commitment. The drag from idle capital on a fund's overall return is real, and over a long enough horizon it is one of the largest leaks a small fund has.

There is no perfect equilibrium between the two. The best I have managed in a long career is to keep both sides close, with a small lean toward more capital than I need for next month's deals, and to keep my referral sources warm enough that the deal flow remains dependable. The lean toward extra capital is not free, but the alternative, turning away a deal because the cash is committed elsewhere, is equally bad. Once a referral source watches you pass on their deal because you ran out of money, they go find a manager who will not run out of money on the next one. Getting them back is harder than keeping them.

The Waterfall

The deal waterfall is the schedule of cash moving through the fund. Capital coming in from new subscriptions. Capital going out for new deals. Cash returning from payoffs and dispositions. Distributions going out to investors. Redemption requests coming in from investors who unexpectedly need liquidity for Little Timmy's braces. The waterfall does not run on the manager's plan. It runs on whatever the market, investors, and the borrowers actually do.

My best-planned month is the month one investor calls with an unexpected redemption request, a borrower whose payoff was supposed to fund three new deals takes another forty-five days to sell, and a new investor who committed $200,000 does not wire by the agreed date. Each of those events on its own is manageable. All three landing in the same week is a fund manager's bad day, and bad days happen.

Managing the waterfall is one of the parts of fund management nobody trains for and everybody learns on the job. Build a reserve. Maintain a relationship with a credit facility that can carry a short-term gap if you need it. Keep the investor communication current so a redemption request is not the first signal you receive that an investor is going to need money. And do not commit to a new deal on capital that has not landed in your operating account. We will come back to that last point at the end of the chapter.

Manager Compensation, Related-Party Transactions, and Disclosures

The manager's compensation structure shapes the way the manager behaves under pressure. A flat management fee on assets under management gives the manager an incentive to keep raising capital regardless of whether good deals are available. Performance fees pull the manager toward chasing yield, sometimes past the point of comfortable underwriting. The cleanest structure I have seen is a subordinated arrangement, where the manager takes nothing until the investors receive a preferred return, and where the manager sits behind the investors in the payment order. Most small funds use some combination of all three. The mix you see in the PPM is a strong signal of how the manager will behave when the deals get tight.

Related-party transactions and affiliate loans are where small funds get into the most legal trouble. The manager has a personal lending business on the side, or owns a brokerage that sources deals into the fund, or controls an entity that borrows from the fund. None of those structures is automatically improper, but each one requires disclosure in the PPM, fair-market-value pricing on every individual transaction, and contemporaneous documentation showing the terms were ones an arm's-length counterparty would have accepted. A related-party loan that is fairly priced and properly disclosed is a manageable structure. The same loan, unpriced and undisclosed, is a fraud claim waiting to be filed.

The disclosures in the PPM are the manager's protection. They are also the investor's protection. If a related-party transaction is going to exist, name it. Describe it. Price it the way the market would price it. Document the pricing. The disclosure does not eliminate the underlying risk. It does mean the question is answered before someone has to ask it.

Concentration and the Single Position That Hurts

A small fund's most predictable failure area is concentration. One borrower with several loans. One submarket. One product type. One asset class. The pool was built loan by loan, and somewhere along the way the manager stopped looking at the portfolio as a whole. A single bad loan in a diversified pool is a write-down the fund absorbs without breaking stride. The same bad loan in a concentrated pool is a liquidity event, because the loss represents a large enough percentage of the pool's capital to interrupt distributions, trigger redemption requests, or force the manager to liquidate other positions at the wrong time.

Cross-collateralization within the fund is its own issue. Pledging the fund's claim on Property A against the borrower's obligations on Property B can strengthen the position. It can also entangle the workout on either loan in the resolution of the other. Cross-collateralization is only a tool. Use it where it makes sense, and document it in the loan files and in your own records so the next manager, or your own counsel, can see what was done and why.

The single-large-position risk on a small fund is the one I worry about most. A loan that represents 20% of the fund's capital base is one borrower's problem away from a fund-level crisis. The deal may look very strong, and the borrower may be solid, but the math of a 20% position going wrong is devastating to a fund. Set concentration limits before the deals come in. Then stick to them when the next big deal walks through the door.

NAV, Audits, and Investor Reporting

Fund accounting on a private lending fund is not the same as accounting on a single property. The fund holds loans with accruing interest, occasional escrow advances, periodic principal paydowns, occasional payoffs, and sometimes a nonperforming asset whose value is now below its carry. The net asset value calculation has to honestly reflect what each of those positions is actually worth. Carrying a nonperforming loan at par because the manager does not want to take the markdown in this quarter's report is one of the small fund's most common quiet failures.

An annual audit by an independent CPA familiar with private credit funds is the protection against that kind of failure. The audit forces the manager to confront the carry of every position, defend the valuation, and stand behind the number that goes on the investor statement. Audits cost real money. They are also the single most cost-effective piece of operational discipline a fund can buy. Skip the audit and the manager is the only check on the manager.

Investor reporting is the manager's chance to set expectations correctly every quarter. Tell the investors what the portfolio looks like, what changed since the last report, which loans paid off, which loans are in workout, and what the manager is doing about it. Bad news told early lands better than bad news told late. Bad news that the investor finds out on their own lands worst of all. Investors do not expect perfect results. They expect honest results, communicated like an adult to an adult.

Credit Infrastructure for a Downturn

The structural protections that hold up a large institutional fund through a downturn do not always scale down to a small fund. The institutional fund has a separate credit committee, a separate workout group, a separate compliance officer, and a separate audit function. The small fund has the manager. When the downturn arrives, the manager is the credit committee, the workout group, the compliance officer, and the audit function all at once.

The infrastructure that compensates for that is the team the manager builds around the fund. A competent securities attorney for the offering. A competent loan attorney for the documents. An independent CPA for the audit and a different CPA for the tax work. A trusted servicer for the loans. An asset manager for the REO. A credit officer reviewing the underwriting on every loan before it funds. Most small managers do not build all of that. The funds that survive a downturn are the ones that had most of it in place before the downturn arrived.

We will cover the broader question of building a practice that lasts in Chapter 23. A fund is a practice with leverage. Everything Chapter 23 says about discipline, infrastructure, and the team applies to a fund, and the amplification of pooled capital makes the consequences of skipping any of it that much larger.

Dougie Downer

Raising capital for a fund is hard. Don't commit capital based on the verbal commitment of an investor until you see money hit your account. It's amazing how many potential investors talk a good game but get alligator arms when it's time to reach for the checkbook.

Chapter 22

Licensing, Usury, and Regulatory Exposure

The line between a private business purpose loan and a regulated consumer loan is thinner than most private lenders and note buyers understand, and the consequences of crossing it are not proportionate to the error. The same is true for the licensing thresholds that separate making a loan from operating as a lender, a broker, or a servicer. Regulators do not care whether you knew the rule applied. They care whether the rule applied. A small operator who crossed the line by accident faces the same enforcement framework as a large operator who crossed it deliberately, and the fines, restitution orders, and license revocations come down on the small operator with disproportionate force. This chapter is the one I would hand to a new private lender or note buyer before I would let them write their first loan.

Business Purpose Versus Consumer

The cleanest line you can draw in this space is the line between a business purpose loan and a consumer loan. A business purpose loan is a loan to a business entity, secured by an asset acquired or held for investment, with the proceeds used for the business rather than for the borrower's personal household. A consumer loan is a loan to a natural person for a personal, family, or household purpose. Federal and state law treat the two very differently. Truth in Lending, RESPA, the high-cost loan triggers, the disclosure regime, and most of the licensing requirements at both the federal and state level were written for consumer lending. Most of them either do not apply to a true business purpose loan, or apply with far lighter touch.

The problem is that the line is drawn on substance, not form. Putting the words "for business purposes" on a note does not make the loan a business purpose loan. The regulator and the courts will look at the actual use of the proceeds, the borrower's intent, the property type, the occupancy, the documentation in the file, and the conduct around the transaction. A loan to an LLC secured by a rental property the borrower actually moves into is a consumer loan dressed up as a business loan, and the regulator will treat it that way...as a consumer loan. A loan to a natural person to refinance an investment property may or may not be a business purpose loan depending on the facts. The default position for a private lender, especially a new one, should be to limit lending to true business purpose loans made to entities with personal guarantors on investment property the borrower will not occupy. That is the cleanest place to operate, and it is the place where the regulatory perimeter sits at its furthest distance.

I will tell on myself here. When Dodd-Frank was first enacted, I threw a hissy fit. I asked everyone within earshot what politicians knew about lending. The answer is that they knew very little, and the statute reflects it. Parts of Dodd-Frank are a mess. The statute did do one useful thing, though. It forced bad actors in consumer lending to be more honest than they had been and it got many bad actors out of the business. It is not how I would have written the rules, but several elements of the framework did help protect consumers. It also protects honest lenders from the bad ones. There is a reason most private lending funds steer well clear of consumer lending. The regulatory exposure is real, the penalties are large, and the operational requirements to do consumer lending properly are not the kind of thing a small fund can absorb. If you are going to be a private lender, limit yourself to business purpose loans to entities with guarantors. When you start lending to consumers, you cross into a different industry.

State Licensing Thresholds

State licensing is where most private lenders first discover they were already out of compliance. Each state draws its own line on when a lender, a broker, or a buyer of loans needs a license, and the lines do not match from state to state. Some states license the originator. Some states license the buyer of the loan. Some states license the broker who refers the loan. Some states license the servicer. Some states license all of them. A handful of states draw a quiet line that catches operators most assume they are clear of.

Years ago, when buying nonperforming loans started to become more mainstream, I was on a panel at an industry conference. Four fund managers, including me, were on stage. The moderator went down the line and asked us to introduce ourselves. The first guy was from a fund whose name I will not mention because they are one of the biggest in the world. He opened with $4.4 billion under management. The next manager had $1.3 billion. The next had $1.1 billion. Then they came to me. I said that I was Doug Smith with Castle Rock and that we do not disclose our assets under management. The other three smirked, because I was the smallest operator on stage by a wide margin. I will admit I was a bit intimidated by the names sitting next to me.

We got the softball questions for the first stretch of the panel, with the other guys throwing around Wall Street buzz words. Then the audience Q&A began. The first questioner was an active real estate investor from Atlanta. He was struggling to find good foreclosure deals and asked how he could start buying nonperforming loans instead. I asked him if all of his business was in Georgia. He said it was. I explained that the Georgia Department of Banking and Finance requires licensing to buy loans, not just to originate them, and that the state draws the line tighter than most. You can buy a note or two, but you cannot do it at scale without the license. I looked to my left, and the other three managers were whispering to each other. *Did you know that? I did not know that.* The truth is, they knew how to raise capital. They did not know how to deploy it in this space, they did not know how to manage it in this space, and they did not know the regulatory environment they were operating in. Their funds were already exposed to large fines, and they had no idea.

Two things came out of that day. I stopped being intimidated by the big guys. And I confirmed, in a very public way, that you have to know the regulatory environment of the space you operate in. Fines can be expensive, license revocations can be fatal to your business, and you can get shut down quite easily for not knowing rules that are written down and publicly available.

NMLS and Owner-Occupied Residential

A separate set of rules applies the moment the collateral is owner-occupied residential property. Loans secured by an owner-occupied one-to-four-family dwelling sit inside the federal mortgage loan originator framework. NMLS licensing applies. The SAFE Act applies. State mortgage broker and mortgage lender licensing applies. The originator on that loan must be a licensed mortgage loan originator, the company the originator works through must be a licensed mortgage broker or mortgage lender, and the loan itself has to be documented under the consumer disclosure regime that came out of the same legislation. There is no exemption for a private lender.

I have an NMLS license, both personally and for the company. We do engage in consumer lending alongside our commercial and investor lending. Most of the readers of this book are not licensed and have no intention of becoming licensed. Licensing comes with strict rules and regulations, and as we have said before, if you are out of compliance, you are out of business. Missing a rule here or there is easy to do, and it can be catastrophic to a small operator. Know the licensing requirements for the type of lending you plan to engage in. If you are lending to consumers on consumer-use property, you are going to need a license. Period. If you are a smaller operator doing a loan to XYZ, LLC, on an investment property, you may be able to operate without the NMLS license, but you are still going to face state and federal usury laws, sometimes state lender licensing rules, and the rest of the regulatory perimeter. Know your licensing requirements before you fund the first deal, not after.

Usury

Usury caps vary by state, by loan type, by borrower type, and by the structure of the transaction. Some states have a general usury cap with statutory exceptions for licensed lenders, for business purpose loans, for loans above a certain dollar threshold, or for loans secured by certain kinds of collateral. Some states have separate caps for consumer loans and for commercial or business purpose loans. A few states have functionally no cap on commercial loans to entities. Federal law sets its own ceilings in certain categories. The rules do not match across state lines, and the interplay between state and federal law is not always intuitive.

We were recently in discussions with a family office about capital for a private lending fund. They came back and told us they were also evaluating another group that was promising significantly higher returns on similar loans. The numbers the other group was advertising were beyond the range you can hit lending inside applicable usury limits in the states they were lending in. As I have said before, the math did not math. Either the other group was lending outside the usury caps and did not know it, or they were lending outside the usury caps and did know it, or the numbers they were marketing were not the numbers the loans were actually producing. None of the three is a story I would want to be told as an investor after the fact. If you are lending in a market, learn the usury limits for the kinds of loans you are doing. Federal law applies, state law applies, and the penalties for crossing a usury cap range from forfeiture of the interest, to forfeiture of the principal, to criminal exposure in a small number of states. Not knowing the cap is not a defense.

HOEPA is the federal high-cost loan framework that sits on top of consumer mortgage lending. It is not going to apply to the readers of this book in any meaningful way, because business purpose loans on investment property are outside its perimeter. If you find yourself near a HOEPA conversation, you are already on the wrong side of the consumer line, and HOEPA is not your largest problem.

Broker, Servicer, and Debt Collector Licensing

The licensing perimeter does not end at the lender. State laws separately license loan brokers, loan servicers, and in many states debt collectors. A private lender or note buyer who places a loan, services a loan, or attempts to collect on a defaulted loan can fall inside one or more of these regimes depending on the state. The trap is that the operator usually does not realize the activity triggers a separate license until a regulator opens an inquiry.

In an earlier chapter, I told you that we do direct work with our borrowers. You have to watch how you interact with borrowers, because there are licensing requirements for servicers, and informal contact can pull an unlicensed operator inside the servicer perimeter. When we hold loans, we use a licensed servicer for most functions. We insist on managing the items we know we do better than the servicer, including working with the foreclosure attorneys and approving workouts. For the regulatory required functions, we use the servicer, and we work through someone at the servicing company to administer those functions. We never intervene on a performing loan. We do monitor the activity of the servicer very, very closely. We also have a long history in this part of the business, and a number of the activities we handle directly require licensing that the average note investor cannot justify the cost of obtaining. If you are not licensed at the level your activity requires, you have to use someone who is.

The same logic applies to brokers and debt collectors. If you refer loans for compensation in a state that licenses loan brokers, the broker license applies. If you collect on a defaulted loan in a state with a debt collector licensing regime, the debt collector license applies. The fact that the loan is yours, that the borrower is in default, or that the activity feels informal does not change the analysis. The activity triggers the license.

When a Note Becomes a Security

The last regulatory line worth knowing is the line where a note becomes a security under state or federal securities law. The Reves test at the federal level, and various state law analogs, look at the motivation of the seller and the buyer, the way the note was marketed, the plan of distribution, the existence of any risk-reducing regulatory regime, and the reasonable expectations of the investor. A single business purpose mortgage sold from one investor to another is usually not a security. A pool of notes marketed and sold in a structured offering, with investors expecting a return generated by the manager's effort, often is. The line is fact specific, and operators who assume their note sale is not a securities transaction are sometimes wrong.

The exposure on this one cuts both ways. The seller of an unregistered security faces rescission, civil penalties, and in some cases criminal liability. The buyer of an unregistered security may have a claim against the seller for years after the sale. Both sides should know what they are doing before the transaction closes. A securities attorney should look at any note sale or pool transaction that is not a single one-off transfer between two seasoned investors. The cost of the legal opinion is small compared to the cost of being on the wrong side of an enforcement action.

The Mad Lender Point of View

The point of view I have settled on over a long career is that you operate inside the rules, not around them. The private lending and note investing space attracts a fair number of operators who treat regulatory compliance as an obstacle to be routed around rather than as a perimeter to be respected. That posture works until it does not. When it stops working, it stops working at a scale that takes the entire operation down with it. I have seen funds shut down for licensing failures the manager could have cured for a few thousand dollars on the front end. I have seen note buyers pay back interest, principal, and penalties on loans they bought without realizing the state required a license to buy them.

Know the licensing rules for every activity you engage in. Know the usury caps in every state you lend in. Know whether your transactions are securities transactions. Hire the legal help you need to know all of this with confidence, and pay the cost of compliance on the front end. The cost of operating inside the rules is one of the lowest cost line items in this business. The cost of operating outside the rules, by accident or otherwise, is sometimes the cost of the business itself.

Dougie Downer

"We are not a bank" has never been a successful defense in the history of lending regulation. Every regulator who has heard it has proceeded anyway.

Part Six

The Long Game

Part Six is about the operating habits that keep a lender or note investor in business through more than one cycle. The technical material across the previous twenty-two chapters covers the credit decision, the structure, the documentation, the workout, and the special situations. None of that produces a practice that lasts without the habits behind it, the willingness to decline a deal that should not be made, and the team built around the lanes where the operator's own competence ends.

The chapters that follow tie the operating side together. By the end of Part Six the reader should understand the point the book has been making since the opening chapter. The credit decision is the product. Everything else either supports it or gets in the way.

Chapter 23

Building a Private Lending and Note Investing Practice That Lasts

The lenders and note investors who survive every cycle share a small number of recognizable habits. They have a written credit policy. They underwrite every loan or every note the same way every time. They monitor their portfolio. They pay professionals to do the work they are not personally equipped to do well. None of it is glamorous, and most of it is invisible to the outside world right up until the moment a downturn proves who built the back end of an operation and who did not. This chapter is about what that back end actually looks like, in plain terms, at the scale a private lender or note investor really operates at.

Your Written Credit Policy

A written credit policy is the document that tells you, before a deal lands on your desk, what you will and will not lend on, how you will price it, how you will document it, and what you will do when something goes sideways. Every regulated lender has one because the regulators require it. The individual private lender or note investor needs one more urgently than a large institution does, not less. The large institution has committees, audit functions, and personnel rotation that catch drift over time. You do not. The only thing standing between your operation and the next bad decision you almost made is the discipline of a written policy that forced you to stop and ask whether the deal in front of you fits the box you said you would lend in.

The policy does not need to be long, but it does need to cover the basics. Those basics include the approved product types you will lend on, the geographic footprint you will operate in, LTV and combined LTV ceilings by product, credit standards, income and capacity standards, borrower entity requirements, documentation requirements, reserve and liquidity standards, your pricing framework, concentration limits by borrower and by product and by geography and by collateral type, an exception policy along with who has authority to approve an exception, servicing standards, and default and workout standards. The policy is the place where you commit, on paper, to the standards you intend to operate to. When a deal comes in that sits outside the policy, you either decline it or you log it as an exception and take it through whatever exception process you committed to.

LOM and Credit Memo Discipline on Every Transaction

I covered this at length in Chapter 12, and I am going to repeat the headline here because it is the single most important habit in this business. Every loan you fund, every note you buy, and every workout you negotiate should be supported by a written loan officer memorandum that lays out the borrower, the collateral, the structure, the income and capacity analysis, the credit, the exit, and the risks. Scale the depth to the size of the operation. Do not scale the standard. A two-page memo on a small fix-and-flip loan and a twelve-page memo on a million-dollar bridge loan can both meet the same standard if the content tracks the substance of the deal. What you cannot do is fund or buy without a memo at all, and what you cannot do is write the memo after the fact to justify a decision you already made. Memos keep you honest. They remind you of things you might miss. After thirty-five years and thousands of loans underwritten, I still do it on every deal. It keeps me steady and my credit quality high.

Concentration Management

Concentration is the silent killer in a private lending or note portfolio. I touched on this in Chapter 14 from the underwriting side. From the portfolio side, the rule is the same. You manage concentration by borrower, by product, by geography, and by collateral type. You set the limits in your credit policy before you have the problem, and you enforce them when the volume actually starts to come in. The pressure to break a concentration limit is always strongest at the worst time, usually when a known borrower brings you the third or fourth or fifth deal in a row and the relationship starts to feel like a strength rather than a risk.

I left the large banks for community banks at a point in my career when I wanted more direct control of the relationships I was managing. The tradeoff was straightforward. I had more autonomy. I had fewer resources. The single ceiling I bumped my head against most often at the community bank level was the legal lending limit. A bank's legal lending limit is the largest single loan the bank is permitted to make under its regulatory capital structure. A bank's exposure limit is the largest aggregate exposure the bank is allowed to carry to any one customer, any one sector, or any one geography. The whole point of those limits is to force the bank to spread the risk it carries. As a private lender, you will struggle even more than a community bank to spread your own risk profile. Imagine a private lender who only made loans in the Lower Ninth Ward of New Orleans in 2005. That operator would have faced two problems at once. The first was potential fair lending exposure for restricting activity to a small geographic pocket of the city. The second was that on August 29 of that year, the entire collateral pool was wiped out by Hurricane Katrina. A sustainable lending practice cannot afford to put all of its eggs in one basket.

Capital Partners and Warehouse Relationships

The infrastructure behind a sustainable lending practice extends well past your own balance sheet. Most operators who scale do so through some combination of capital partners, fund investors, warehouse lines, table funding relationships, and back-end note buyers. Each of those introduces its own due diligence requirements, reporting requirements, covenants, and economic terms. The capital does not show up at the right cost or in the right size unless you have built the relationship, demonstrated the track record, and put the documentation in place to support the structure. Capital will not simply arrive once you decide to raise it.

When I first set up our company, we paid for a Regulation D offering and assumed raising capital from accredited investors would be the easy part. I was wrong. I kissed a lot of frogs. The vast majority of the people I spoke to in that first round talked a great game about investing meaningful capital into the offering, and then developed alligator arms when they tried to reach for their checkbook. Verbal commitments do not fund deals. Money that has cleared into your bank account funds deals. Until you have the money under your own control, you do not have the money. Do not commit to buying a note or funding a loan against capital you have been promised but have not yet received. Take that one from somebody who learned it the hard way a long time ago. People talk a good game. Very few of them come through.

The Team You Build Around Yourself

A private lending or note investing practice is held together by the team you place around the operation. You might even serve in one or more of these capacities. You need a competent underwriter. You need a real estate attorney with experience in the products you lend on and in the states you lend in. You need a title agent who knows how to clear a difficult title issue and not just write a policy on a clean one. You need a servicer who will actually follow your instructions on the loans you keep. You need an insurance agent who understands force-placed coverage and lender's loss payee endorsements. You need a CPA who can tell you how the entity structure you operate under interacts with the reporting and tax treatment of your loan and note portfolio. If you intend to take capital from self-directed IRAs, you need IRA custodian relationships, and you need to understand the prohibited transaction rules under section 4975 of the Internal Revenue Code well enough to keep your investors out of trouble.

The first business-for-self borrower I ever looked at was when I was around twenty-one years old. I was at my first job out of college. I was a baby banker with an accounting degree and not much practical context for what I was looking at. I had been trained to underwrite W-2 income from paystubs, and I was good at that piece. The borrower provided me with a W-2 showing $120,000 in wages. That was real money thirty-five years ago. I took the file to my manager and asked for a loan approval. He asked me whether I had asked for the tax returns. The borrower owned the business. I had not asked for the returns, because the W-2 looked clean and I did not yet understand why I would need anything else. I went back and asked for the returns. The borrower had personally been paid $120,000. The business had lost $160,000 that same year. That lesson stayed with me. I was a smart kid with an accounting degree, but I did not know what I did not know. That is the most dangerous place to operate from in this business.

Most of the readers of this book are not coming at private lending from a formal credit background. You may be coming from real estate, from investing, from construction, from law, from running a small business of your own, or from any one of a hundred other places. When my car breaks down, I take it to a mechanic, because the mechanic knows things about cars that I do not. When I get sick, I go to a doctor, because the doctor knows the human body better than I do. Credit is no different. If you are not coming at this from a position of formal credit training, you will miss things you do not yet know you are missing. The right move is to bring in help from someone who has done this work for a long time. There is a small market of seasoned credit officers and senior underwriters who consult into private lending operations for exactly this reason, and the cost of that help is very small next to the cost of the loans you would have written without it.

Knowing the Edges of Your Own Competence

Every operator I respect in this business knows where their own competence ends, and builds around the edges they cannot cover themselves. The operators who get into trouble are almost always operators who refused to admit there was an edge.

Having the ability to pull a consumer credit report is reserved for parties who have been vetted by the credit reporting agencies. Every year, I have to go through a fairly stringent audit to keep that access. The bureaus do an office visit, which now happens virtually rather than in person. One year, I had a 55-inch television on the wall of my office, because I work weekends and like to have the game on while I am working. The auditor told me I had to take it down. No televisions in the office. Another year, I had a set of dumbbells in the corner of the office, and was told to remove those as well. No gym equipment in the office. The point is not the television or the dumbbells. The point is that whether you are setting up to pull credit, to be licensed to service loans in a particular state, or to operate in any one of the regulated lanes of this business, the access comes with hurdles you have to clear and ongoing costs you have to absorb. You have to do it right, every year, or the access goes away.

As an NMLS-licensed company, we have access to underwriting and origination tools that are not available to most private lenders who do not carry the licensing. We pay for them, and we use them every day. If you are setting up a private lending operation and you do not have access to those tools, either because the licensing does not fit your model or the cost does not justify itself at your scale, you have to think through the workarounds before you fund your first loan. What loan origination software will you use to manage your pipeline? What secure portal will you use for borrowers to upload bank statements, tax returns, and identification documents? How will you handle the data retention and information security requirements that come along with handling that material? None of that is glamorous. It is the difference between an operation that can actually take in deals and process them properly, and an operator who is collecting borrower documents in personal email and hoping nothing breaks.

Growing at a Sustainable Pace

The last habit on the list is restraint about pace. The temptation in a growing private lending practice is to take every deal that meets the credit standard, raise capital as fast as the deals can absorb it, and build the back end on the fly. Operators who grow that way tend to falter.

I was sitting at my desk at Wachovia one afternoon when one of the business bankers wandered into my office to say hi. He saw a picture of my then fiancee, now my wife, on the credenza. He looked at the picture, looked at me, and said, "That is who you are marrying? You really outkicked your coverage." He was right. I married well out of my league, and for reasons passing understanding, it has worked out for me. In business, you cannot afford to outkick your coverage. In football, a punter is not just judged on how far the ball goes. The punter is judged on hang time, which is how long the ball is in the air before the returner can catch it. Hang time gives the coverage team time to get downfield and make a play. If a punter kicks the ball too far, the returner has time to find blockers and run the punt back the other way for a long gain. That is what it means to outkick your coverage. The same principle applies in a private lending business. You grow at the pace your infrastructure can actually absorb. When the production side is writing more deals than the underwriting and servicing side can handle, you do not have a good problem on your hands. You have an underwriting and servicing problem dressed up as a sales success. Slow the production side down until the back end catches up, or build the back end out before you open the production side back up. Finding the balance between the two is the actual job of running this business.

The Mad Lender Point of View

The lenders and note investors I have watched survive every cycle over a long career did not survive because they were the smartest people in the business. They survived because they had a written credit policy, they underwrote every deal the same way, they managed concentration, they paid for the help they needed in the places they were not strongest, and they grew at a pace their infrastructure could actually support. The operators who blew up did not blow up because the market turned. They blew up because the market turned and exposed the things they had not bothered to build. Build the back end of your operation first. The loans you write after that are the loans that will hold up.

Dougie Downer

Every private lender and every note investor who has taken a significant loss in this business believed they were being careful. Careful is a process. You do not know what you do not know. Surround yourself with strong, knowledgeable professionals and pay them what their help is worth. To do otherwise is foolish.

Chapter 24

The Word No

The hardest decision in private lending and note investing is not what to fund or what to buy. It is what to decline. The yes is the fun part of the business. The yes produces income, builds the pipeline, and keeps the operation moving. The no is harder. The no is the part of the business that protects the income, the pipeline, and the operation from the loans that would have damaged all three. Operators who cannot bring themselves to say no do not remain operators for long.

The Real Cost of a Yes That Should Have Been a No

Every loan that should have been declined and was funded anyway costs the lender across several dimensions at once. The capital is the most obvious cost. The principal is at risk, and the recovery from a poorly structured loan that defaults is almost always less than the recovery from a soundly structured loan that defaults. The time is the next cost. The hours the operator and the team spend on a problem loan come out of the hours available to work on the rest of the portfolio. The management capacity is the third cost. Every troubled loan in the file demands attention disproportionate to the income that loan was ever going to produce, and that attention is no longer available for the loans that would have produced income without trouble. The reputation is the fourth cost, and the quietest. Borrowers, brokers, investors, and capital partners watch how a lender handles trouble. A portfolio with chronic trouble starts to attract the kind of business that gravitates toward operators with chronic trouble.

I told the community bank board member story in Chapter 1, and it belongs here as well. The loan had been declined by me. The board member personally believed in the borrower and the project, funded the million dollars out of his own pocket, and lost every dollar of it. The lesson is not that he was foolish. The lesson is that he overrode a no that had already been delivered by someone whose job was to deliver it, and the override cost him a million dollars. My no was not a personal judgment. It was a credit judgment. He converted the credit judgment into a personal one, and the loss followed. Most of the worst losses I have seen in private lending and note investing come the same way. Someone overrode a no that had already been given, by themselves or by someone they trusted, because the relationship or the story or the upside felt too important to walk away from.

Saying No When You Were Raised to Say Yes

I grew up in a Midwestern farm town, and the culture I was raised in was a culture of helping. When somebody was sick or somebody in the family passed away, you took food over to the house. You looked out for each other. There was real trust in that. We also did not want to put each other out. You were self-sufficient, you did not ask for help unless you had to, and when somebody else asked for help, you gave it. That was simply how it worked. When I went to college, I carried that posture with me, and I had not yet learned to say no.

One day a guy in my fraternity asked to borrow my car. I handed him the keys without thinking twice about it, because that is what you do where I come from. The next time I went to get into the car, the interior was completely trashed. I had never learned to say no, and it cost me a few hours of cleaning. That is small compared to what private lending will teach you on the same point. If you came from a background that valued helping, or you came from a profession that trained you to find a way to yes, you have to deliberately retrain yourself in this business. Declining a deal is not a failure of character. It is part of the job.

A Quick No Is Better Than a Long Maybe

I cannot recall the last time anyone gave me grief over a quick no. When you know your business and you do not see a path to getting the deal done, a quick no is always better than a long maybe. Newer lenders want to be all things to all people. You cannot be. I appreciate a challenge, but you cannot tell a borrower it is not a problem when you think it actually might be a problem. If you do, you spend the next thirty days white-knuckling it, trying to figure out how to pull off what you already told the borrower would be easy. One of two things happens. Either you pull it off, and the borrower still had a rocky experience that did not match what you promised, or you do not pull it off, and the borrower you were so positive with tells everybody who will listen what a terrible lender you are. Neither outcome is worth the effort.

Sir Richard Branson has been quoted as saying something to the effect that when somebody presents you with an opportunity and you do not know how to do it, you should accept the challenge and figure it out. Branson is more accomplished than I am, and questioning his logic from where I sit feels presumptuous. That said, Mount Everest is littered with the bodies of climbers who thought they could pull it off. In this business, when you take on a deal you have no idea how to execute, you are toying with somebody's plans, somebody's hopes, and somebody's dreams. Do not tell a borrower you can do something if you do not know how you are going to do it. A quick no is better than a long maybe, and the borrower will respect the quick no long after they would have forgiven the long maybe.

Declining Family, Friends, and Trusted Referrals

The hardest declines in this business are not the cold deals where you have no connection to the applicant. The hardest declines are the deals that come from a family member, a long-time friend, or a referral source you have known for years. Those declines are hard because the no follows the relationship. The no comes home with you. It shows up at Thanksgiving, at the next business dinner, at the next time you see the referring broker in the lobby of a closing. The relationship and the credit decision get tangled together, and untangling them takes deliberate effort.

The first thing you have to keep clear in your own head is that the credit decision is a credit decision and the relationship is a relationship. A loan that should not be made does not become a loan that should be made because the borrower is a family member. The collateral does not become better collateral because the broker is somebody you have closed twenty loans with. The capacity does not become real capacity because the borrower's grandfather and your grandfather went to high school together. The credit decision and the relationship are separate matters that you manage with the same honesty you would expect from anyone else in the same situation.

The second thing is that family and friends will respect you more, not less, for declining cleanly. The brother-in-law who is told no by his sister's husband may grumble, but he will grumble far more when the loan he wanted goes bad and his sister's husband is the lender who let him into it. Bad loans inside a family do not stay loans for long. They become arguments. They become silence at the dinner table. They become wedges that outlast the loan itself.

Using the Underwriter as the Structural Buffer

This is one of the most underused tools in the private lending business. The credit decision sits with the underwriter. The relationship sits with the lender. The two can be deliberately separated, with the lender holding the relationship and the underwriter delivering the no. Done well, the relationship survives the no, and the underwriter absorbs the friction that would otherwise have come to rest on the lender.

We do this for our clients on a fairly regular basis. Some of the smaller fund managers and private lenders we work with find themselves in a position where a loan they really do not want to do has been brought to them by somebody they cannot socially decline. One of our clients had a brother-in-law come to him with a deal. The idea the borrower had was, in plain terms, a bad one. The borrower was convinced it was the greatest idea anyone had ever had. Our client, correctly, identified it as a decline. Declining it personally would have made Thanksgiving awkward, so I declined it on his behalf. The line our client used afterward was simple. "I would have done it. That old so-and-so Doug would not let me do it." The deal did not happen. Thanksgiving was fine. The relationship was intact. The credit decision was correct. I was the designated jerk.

Sometimes it is hard to say no. It is acceptable to get help saying it. That is a feature of building a real team around the operation, not a weakness. The lender who insists on personally delivering every no, in every conversation, with every relationship, will eventually fund a loan that should have been declined because the conversation was too uncomfortable to have. A lender who built a team to deliver the difficult nos when needed gets the benefit of the decline without the cost of the conversation.

What a Clean Decline Sounds Like

A professional decline closes the door without bruising the relationship. The conversation has three parts. First, the decline itself, delivered without ambiguity. Second, the credit reason for the decline, in plain terms, without lecture. Third, a clear ending, with no false hope and no extended maybe.

The decline itself sounds like, "I am not going to be able to do this loan." It does not sound like, "I do not think I can do this loan." It does not sound like, "Let me see if I can find a way." It does not sound like, "This is a tough one." The decline has to be the decline. If you hedge it, the borrower hears the hedge and holds onto it for the next month.

The credit reason should be honest, short, and operationally framed. "The capacity is not there to service this debt under the structure you are asking for." "The collateral position behind the senior lien does not give me enough cushion at the loan amount you are asking for." "The credit history does not support an unsecured personal guarantee at this size." The borrower may not like the reason, but the borrower will respect the reason. Lectures are not respected. Operational reasons are.

The ending should close the door cleanly. "If something changes on the capacity side, I would be willing to take another look. Until then, this is not a loan I am going to make." That gives the borrower a real path back if the underlying facts actually change, and it gives them nothing to chew on if the facts do not. False hope is the cruelty most newer lenders cannot resist. Real respect for the borrower means giving them the honest no and letting them go find the right lender, or the right project, somewhere else.

A realtor who refers business to our mortgage company came to us to buy a property of his own. He loves cars, and I mean really, really loves cars. He had a long list of auto loans across his collection of toys, and the monthly debt service on those loans was killing his debt-to-income ratio. We could not do the loan as the file sat. I gave him the no quickly. I delivered it with empathy and I walked him through the math, line by line, so he understood why. About a year later, he came back. He had listened. He had taken it to heart. He had decided on his own that he could not afford that much debt for his toys, and he had liquidated most of his automotive holdings. His debt-to-income ratio was now in line. We put a loan together for him on the property he wanted. The no was not the end of the relationship. The no was the start of the conversation that produced the right loan a year later, with a borrower who had earned his way to it.

The Mad Lender Point of View

I have made my share of mistakes in this business. The mistakes I regret most are the loans I funded after I had already decided in my own head that I did not want to make them. Every one of those started with a yes that should have been a no, delivered to a borrower I liked, on a deal I had already underwritten to a decline. The mistakes I do not regret are the deals I walked away from cleanly. I never lost a dime on a loan I did not make. Neither will you. Build the habit of saying no. Build the team that can deliver the no on your behalf when you need them to. Protect the operation from the deals that should never have been funded in the first place. No is an answer.

Dougie Downer

Every loan that should not have been funded started with somebody saying, "but he is a good person." No is an answer.

Chapter 25

Who You Hire Matters More Than What You Charge

Who you hire matters more than what you charge. The rate sheet does not protect a portfolio. The team behind the rate sheet does. Over the years I have watched dozens of operations move through good markets and rough markets, and the operations that came through both intact had something in common. They had built a team around the lending function that was capable of catching what the principal could not catch on their own.

The Team Behind a Lending Operation

The team behind a lending operation is rarely visible to anyone outside the business. The CPA who keeps the entity books clean and the tax filings accurate. The attorney who structures the loan documents and shows up when a workout goes sideways. The title agent who clears a difficult title report rather than just writing a clean one on the easy file. The servicer who actually follows your instructions when a loan goes nonperforming. The processor who keeps the file moving without losing anything along the way. The underwriter who reads the file carefully and mitigates your downside risk. Every lending operation has somebody filling those positions. The only question is whether they are filled by somebody who is good at the role, or whether they are filled by somebody who happened to be available when the role came up. That decision, made eight or ten times across the team you put together, shapes the trajectory of the operation more than the rate sheet ever will.

Hire for the Right Fit, Not for the Right Resume

When our mortgage company was young, I needed a good processor. Rates were climbing at the time, the refinance shops around the country were laying off staff in large numbers, and the job I posted drew over three hundred resumes. I narrowed the field down to ten interviews. Then a resume that did not match the experience profile of the others caught my eye. The candidate did not have the file count the other applicants had, but I saw a work ethic in her resume that the others did not show. I called her first. I liked her. Every interview I did after that one was fine, but I still liked her better. She joined us, and she is still with us today. Her name is Nancy, and she is a different Nancy from the one earlier in this book. The trust we have built with her did not exist on any of the resumes I read first. It came from hiring for the person, not for the paper.

Every bank I ever worked for required us to take personality assessments, and I hated them right up until I understood them. In lending, the roles are quite different from one another. You have the leaders, you have the sales people, you have the loan officer assistants who keep the relationship moving, and you have the processors who keep the file moving. I have found that personality types on a tool like the DISC profile are good predictors not necessarily of success but of happiness in a given role. Somebody who is happy in the role and has the aptitude for it has a very strong chance of being successful in it. I am a high D on the DISC profile. The highest-producing loan officers I have worked with over the years have generally been high I's. The best loan officer assistants have been high S's. The best processors have been high C's. A high I would be unhappy as a processor, and a high C would struggle with the sales grind that a high I thrives on. Does this hold true for everybody? Of course not. We each have roles we shine at and others we don't. Just because an I might not enjoy processing doesn't mean they are a bad person. It just means they are in the wrong role for them. I believe it was Einstein who pointed out that you can't judge a fish by its ability to climb a tree. The point is that you do not hire for the resume. You hire for the fit, and you treat the person well once they are in the role.

Even the Right Hire Has to Be Monitored

My degree is in accounting, but by the time I started a business of my own, I was so far removed from active accounting work that I hired a CPA to take care of the firm's tax filings. He was a small practitioner when I hired him, and we developed a strong working relationship. Over the years his practice grew, and he started landing clients much larger than I was. I became small potatoes in his book of business, and he handed my file off to underlings. Mistakes started showing up, and IRS letters started hitting my inbox. I called him, sent the letters over, and he said it was no problem and that he would address it. A couple of months later, another letter came in. I called him again, and he did not remember our first conversation at all and had done nothing about it. I sent both letters over again. No problem. He would address it. A couple of months later, another IRS letter, and another call, and he again did not remember the earlier conversations. I eventually had to find somebody else to take over the relationship and clean up the mess.

The lesson is not that he was a bad CPA. The lesson is that even the right hire has to be monitored. A relationship that started with strong service can drift, especially when the firm on the other end of it grows past the client and the work gets handed off to people who do not own the relationship. The lender who hires a professional and then stops paying attention to the work product is going to be surprised at some point by what has been quietly happening underneath them. Pay attention to the work, even when you trust the person doing it.

The Best Working Relationships Become Real Relationships

John is one of the attorneys I have used over the years. He is a scotch-drinking, foul-joke-telling rogue of a guy, which is to say he is my kind of guy. He is also a very good lawyer. If you have been in business for any length of time and you have not been involved in litigation on one side or the other, you are probably not doing enough business. John has stepped in and taken care of us at every turn.

A long time ago, when I was clawing and scratching to make a living, a situation came up that I was not sure how to handle. I called John. He made the problem go away. I called him afterward and asked what I owed him. Knowing things were lean at the time, he said, "That is what friends do for one another." For the record, I took a bottle of scotch over to his office. I never expected the work for free, I will never forget what he did, and I would not presume to ever get something for free again. I would return that favor a hundred times over if he ever needed me to. That, my friends, is a relationship.

The people you bring onto the team around your operation are not vendors. They are the professionals who will keep you out of the kind of trouble that ends operations. The relationships you build with them, over years, are part of the back end of the business. Treat them like the relationships they are, not like line items you might trim next year.

The Cost of Taking Advice from Amateurs

Somebody told me a long time ago that in this country, there are two people you pay no matter what. You pay the IRS, and you pay your attorney. The point of the line, I think, was not really about the IRS or the attorney. The point was that the professional advice you need, you are going to pay for one way or another. You can pay for it on the front end by hiring it, or you can pay for it on the back end through the cost of having operated without it. The cost shows up either way. The cheaper of the two costs, by a very wide margin, is paying for it on the front end.

There are investor groups and online forums in this space where people post specific and technical questions that ought to be put to an attorney, a CPA, or somebody with a credit background. They are looking for the answer for free. The answers they get from the peanut gallery on the internet are usually worth what they paid for them. If you think it is expensive to pay for expert advice, imagine the cost of taking important advice from an amateur. The cost of a single bad decision made on amateur advice will, more often than not, exceed the cost of professional advice across an entire year.

The Mad Lender Point of View

This is the last chapter of the book, and the closing point is also the simplest. Who you hire matters more than what you charge. Over twenty-five chapters, I have written a portion of what I know about how this business actually works, where the losses come from, what protects a portfolio, and what tends to take one apart. All of it is built from a long career of writing loans, buying loans, servicing loans, and working out the ones that did not pay back. The patterns are real. The mistakes are repeatable. The protections are not complicated, but they are not free either.

What you do with what is in this book is up to you. You can spend a career building credit judgment on your own, and accept the losses that come along with that path. You can find people with the judgment already built, bring them onto the team around your operation, and learn from them while they protect you. You can decide that the cost of avoiding losses is not worth the cost of the help, and run the operation accordingly. Different operators land in different places on that question. In my experience, the ones who stay in this business through more than one cycle did not arrive there by accident. They built a team around the operation that allowed them to.

Choose the team carefully. Treat them well. Pay attention to the work after you have hired them. Build relationships that outlast the next cycle. The rest will follow.

Dougie Downer

If you think it is expensive to hire a professional, it is even more expensive to hire an amateur. You will usually need to hire the professional anyway to fix what the amateur left behind.

About the Author

Doug Smith has spent more than thirty-five years as a lending executive with some of the largest banks in the world, community banks, and mortgage companies. He started his career at Norwest in St. Louis in 1991 making collection calls and learning the credit business from the bottom of the lifecycle up. He worked his way through residential mortgage, investor lending, commercial finance, private banking, and distressed assets across roles at Norwest, Bank One, Wachovia, and community banks, completing formal credit training programs along the way.

He was in commercial lending and handled the special assets desk at a community bank through the 2008 cycle. In 2009 he founded what became Castle Rock Capital Management to buy severely delinquent residential and commercial mortgage loans coming out of the bank market. Castle Rock has grown into a private lending and portfolio management company that originates loans through Castle Rock Capital Funding and manages performing and nonperforming portfolios for private clients.

Doug later launched The Mad Lender, a private credit consulting practice. It manages everything from single-deal credit reviews to ongoing retainer relationships covering credit policy, underwriting build-out, and portfolio-level oversight. The clients are private lenders, note investors, fund operators, and self-directed IRA investors who need a credit officer behind their decisions but cannot justify the cost of building one in house. For operators with the capital but no internal credit infrastructure, The Mad Lender also functions as the credit team behind the operation. The Mad Lender brand was built around the observation that most of the operators in this market are capital holders rather than credit people. This book makes the case.

Doug speaks on credit underwriting, workout, and note investing at industry events. He lives in the Tampa Bay area with his wife, an accomplished designer and real estate investor in her own right, and his daughter, an art student at one of the top art schools in the world, who designed the cover art for this book.

www.ingramcontent.com/pod-product-compliance
Ingram Content Group UK Ltd.
Pitfield, Milton Keynes, MK11 3LW, UK
UKHW010008031026
15589UKWH00008B/1542

9 798996 642700